What is Qualitative Interviewing?

'What is?' Research Methods series

Edited by Graham Crow, University of Edinburgh

ISSN: 2048–6812

The 'What is?' series provides authoritative introductions to a range of research methods which are at the forefront of developments in the social sciences. Each volume sets out the key elements of the particular method and features examples of its application, drawing on a consistent structure across the whole series. Written in an accessible style by leading experts in the field, this series is an innovative pedagogical and research resource.

What is Online Research?
Tristram Hooley, Jane Wellens and John Marriott

What is Social Network Analysis?
John Scott

What is Qualitative Research?
Martyn Hammersley

What are Qualitative Research Ethics?
Rose Wiles

What are Community Studies?
Graham Crow

What is Discourse Analysis?
Stephanie Taylor

Forthcoming books:

What is Narrative Research?
Molly Andrews, Mark Davis, Cigdem Esin, Lar-Christer Hyden, Margareta Hyden, Corinne Squire and Barbara Harrison

What is Inclusive Research?
Melanie Nind

What is Quantitative Longitudinal Data Analysis?
Vernon Gayle and Paul Lambert

What is qualitative interviewing?

Rosalind Edwards and Janet Holland

BLOOMSBURY
NEW DELHI • LONDON • OXFORD • NEW YORK • SYDNEY

First published in India 2018
First published 2013

Bloomsbury Academic India
An imprint of Bloomsbury Publishing Plc
BLOOMSBURY, Bloomsbury Academic India and the Diana logo are trademarks of Bloomsbury Publishing Plc

This edition published with permission from Bloomsbury Publishing Plc,
50 Bedford Square, London, WC1B3DP, UK

British Library Cataloguing-in-Publication Data
A catalogue record for this book is available from the British Library.

Library of Congress Cataloging-in-Publication Data
A catalog record for this book is available from the Library of Congress.

ISBN 978 93 88002 29 5
10 9 8 7 6 5
For sale in the Indian subcontinent only

Bloomsbury Publishing India Pvt. Ltd
Second Floor, Building No. 4
DDA Complex LSC, Pocket C – 6 & 7
Vasant Kunj, New Delhi 110070
www.bloomsbury.com

Typeset by Newgen Knowledge Works (P) Ltd., Chennai, India
Printed and bound in India by Replika Press Pvt. Ltd.

Contents

Series foreword

The idea behind this series is a simple one: to provide concise and accessible overviews of a range of frequently-used research methods and of current issues in research methodology. Books in the series have been written by experts in their fields with a brief to write about their subject for a broad audience who are assumed to be interested but not necessarily to have any prior knowledge. The series is a natural development of presentations made in the 'What is?' strand at Economic and Social Research Council Research Methods Festivals which have proved popular both at the Festivals themselves and subsequently as a resource on the website of the ESRC National Centre for Research Methods.

Methodological innovation is the order of the day, and the 'What is?' format allows researchers who are new to a field to gain an insight into its key features, while also providing a useful update on recent developments for people who have had some prior acquaintance with it. All readers should find it helpful to be taken through the discussion of key terms, the history of how the method or methodological issue has developed, and the assessment of the strengths and possible weaknesses of the approach through analysis of illustrative examples.

This sixth book in the series is devoted to qualitative interviewing, which is one of the most widely-used of all research methods in the social sciences. The ubiquity of the interview method is sometimes interpreted as a sign of people choosing a research tool that is no more difficult than engaging in everyday conversation, but such a view would be mistaken, as the authors of this book demonstrate. To do qualitative interviewing well requires clarity of purpose on the part of both the researcher and the people being researched, and it also requires skilful execution by a researcher who has skill, subtlety and sensitivity. In turn this means that qualitative interviewing can take a variety of forms, to be drawn upon according to the many things that make for variation in research objectives and in context. Ros Edwards and Janet Holland's book takes readers through the debates about the nature and purpose of qualitative interviewing, debates that they show are fascinating for both their history and their continuing evolution. What may appear from the outside as an 'easy' method turns out on closer inspection to throw up ethical, theoretical and practical challenges that require sustained engagement if the goal of getting at people's understanding of the social world is to be achieved.

The books cannot provide information about their subject matter down to a fine level of detail, but they will equip readers with a powerful sense of reasons why it deserves to be taken seriously and, it is hoped, with the enthusiasm to put that knowledge into practice.

Graham Crow
Series editor

Tables and figures

Table

Figures

Acknowledgements

This book is the sum of many years of experience of doing qualitative interviews so we would like to thank all the people on whom we have practiced interviewing across the years. We also learned a considerable amount from our qualitative research colleagues. Thanks too to Graham Crow for asking us to write this book and for his continuing interest in the work.

1 What do the key terms used about qualitative interviews mean?

Introduction

Interviews are ubiquitous in everyday life. We have all been interviewed, at school, at university, for jobs, in a medical setting, and seen or read interviews with others. We know the format, what to do and how to do it. Modern society has been called the 'interview', or even the 'confessional' society, the latter calling up a particular type of interview where intimate matters may be revealed (Atkinson and Silverman 1997). Most of us are probably more personally familiar with the role of interviewee, but many of us will have undertaken interviews ourselves, and most of these will have been qualitative interviews in the broadest sense, one person asking another person questions on a particular topic or issue, and the other responding. We will also know from our own experience that these interviews can differ widely, from the confidential probing of the medical interview in a (relatively) private space, through the publicity oriented celebrity interview on screen or in print, to the perhaps aggressive questioning of a politician by a television journalist broadcast in the national news. So clearly both the immediate and broader social contexts are relevant to the way the interview will be conducted, experienced and understood.

In this book we want to move from our everyday experience and understanding of the characteristics of the interview, to the use of the qualitative interview as a methodological and research tool in social science. The interview is probably the most widely used method employed in qualitative research, a central resource for social science. Qualitative interviews have been the basis for many important studies across the range of disciplinary fields, but understandings of what it means to carry out such interviews have shifted over time in line with ebbs and flows in the prominence of particular philosophical approaches to understanding the social world and how it works (discussed in Chapter 2). These ebbs and flows have led to changing conceptions of the researcher: as objective and so able to access objective knowledge about the interviewee and their social world; as implicated in the processes at play in the interview in a range of ways that affect their understanding of the knowledge that can be produced in the interview; or as an advocate speaking for or giving voice to the interviewee. Debates around these issues are explored in this book. A major theme coursing through the book relates to how to approach research and particular methodological tools, such as the qualitative interview that is the focus of this book. In general, the use of a particular method should be derived from the research topic, the research questions to which an answer is sought and the theoretical framework within which the researcher is working. The researcher moves from research concern and topic to research questions, to appropriate method via their underpinning philosophical stance and theoretical approach to understanding the social world, so constructing their methodology (Mason 2002; Ramazanoglu with Holland 2002).

The chapters of the book will describe the different forms that qualitative interviews can take and the kinds of tools or aids to discussion that can be used during interviews, always linking back to the topic and aims of the research being carried out, and its underpinning philosophical approach. The practicalities of qualitative interviewing are as ever undergoing change and challenges with the availability and use of new technologies, but are also subject to enduring issues around asking questions and listening to the answers, and the implications of the underlying power dynamics of broader social relations for research and interviewer – interviewee relations. In this chapter we provide definitions of qualitative interviews and discuss debates about changing descriptions of the interviewee as 'research subject', 'interviewee', 'respondent', or 'participant'. We briefly discuss samples in qualitative interviews and review the changing wider social/economic context in which qualitative interviews are conducted. The chapter sets the scene for the book to follow.

What is a qualitative interview?

Most text books will tell you that interviews range through a continuum, from structured, through semi-structured, to unstructured (or focused) interviews (Bryman 2001, May 1997). The structured interview is at the quantitative end of the scale, and more used in survey approaches. The rest of the scale, semi-structured and unstructured, is the area occupied by qualitative researchers, with the interviews characterized by increasing levels of flexibility and lack of structure. Many of the terms you will have discovered applied to qualitative interviewing appear in this part of the continuum, for example in-depth, informal, non-directed, open-ended, conversational, naturalistic, narrative, biographical, oral or life history, ethnographic and many more discussed in more detail in Chapter 3. The terms used for any particular interview type relate to the underlying philosophy and specific approach taken to research, discussed further in Chapter 2.

Briefly, the structured interview is based on a questionnaire with a sequence of questions, asked in the same order and the same way of all subjects of the research, with little flexibility available to the researcher. The major objective is for neutral interviewers to obtain comparable information from a potentially large number of subjects. It is typical of more positivist approaches, with methodological rules for its practice, and often is subjected to statistical methods of analysis.

A considerable range of qualitative approaches use semi-structured and unstructured interviews, as suggested by the list above. Jennifer Mason argues that, despite the large variations in style and tradition, all qualitative and semi-structured interviewing has certain core features in common:

1. The interactional exchange of dialogue (between two or more participants, in face-to-face or other contexts).
2. A thematic, topic-centred, biographical or narrative approach where the researcher has topics, themes or issues they wish to cover, but with a fluid and flexible structure.
3. A perspective regarding knowledge as situated and contextual, requiring the researcher to ensure that relevant contexts are brought into focus so that the situated knowledge can be produced. Meanings and understandings are created in an interaction, which is effectively a co-production, involving the construction or reconstruction of knowledge. [Adapted from Mason 2002: 62]

With a colleague, one of us has pointed out that as well as being interactional, the interview is a social and potentially a learning event for both participants:

> As a social event it has its own set of interactional rules which may be more or less explicit, more or less recognized by the participants. In addition . . . there are several ways in which the interview

> constitutes a learning process. . . . Participants can discover, uncover or generate the rules by which they are playing this particular game. The interviewer can become more adept at interviewing, in terms of the strategies which are appropriate for eliciting responses. (Holland and Ramazanoglu 1994: 135)

Both interviewers and interviewees can learn more about certain aspects of themselves and the other, with or without this being an explicit part of the interactional exchange. So, who are the players in a qualitative interview?

The changing subject of research

You might have noticed that in writing about interviews earlier we referred to the 'subjects' of the research, and the eagle-eyed will have seen Mason (above) referring to both the researcher and the researched as 'participants'. What those who are being researched are called are not just neutral terms, but also indicate ways of thinking about them and how they are understood as relating to the interview, and consequently reflect the philosophical stance of the researcher. Terms for the researched have included subject, respondent, informant, interviewee and participant, the sequence here suggesting a movement from passive to active. Subject is typical of the close-ended, structured interview, matched by an interviewer who is expected to introduce no biases into the research and data, and deliver objectivity by asking the same questions in the same way of all those who appear for the interview, ignoring as far as possible the subjectivity of the subject. Criticisms of this position come from those who are interested in the views, understandings and subjectivities of the people they research in differing ways, including those who take interpretive, feminist, postmodern, emancipatory and critical realist approaches, all discussed in Chapter 2. Historically, respondent and informant have been associated with ethnographic methods, where key figures are sought when researching particular groups or cultures, to provide useful information on the community being studied. Participant emerges from this field approach too, and applies specifically to the researcher in a method typical of ethnography: participant observation. Here the researcher is still an outsider, although hoping to become more of an insider, or more accepted, by participating in the activities of the group being researched. Interviewee is matched by interviewer, the similarity of terms suggesting more equality in the research relationship. Participant takes this further, and carries with it from feminism and other interpretivist positions certain understandings of the part played by researched and researcher. Participation in research can empower the interviewee, and many feminists have sought to give voice in their research to those, particularly women, who have been unheard or silenced in earlier social science research. From this perspective, reflexivity is called for in the researcher, who must recognize themselves both as part of the research process and the power relations that permeate the research encounter of the qualitative interview (Hammersley 2012). Both researcher and researched bring with them concepts, ideas, theories, values, experiences and multiply intersecting identities, all of which can play a part in research interaction in the qualitative interview.

Changes over time in the terms used for participants in research reflect changes in the underlying philosophical positions adopted. Broadly they chart movement from the notion of the neutral interviewer, standardization and exclusion of bias at the heart of more positivist approaches, to ideas of reflexive construction, difference and shifting positionalities of researcher and researched that have emerged from feminist, postmodern and interpretivist stances. The historical shifting philosophical phases through which this sequence of changes has emerged is outlined in Chapter 2. Throughout this book we use terms such as researcher and interviewer, and interviewee, participant, respondent and subject, according to the context in which they occur.

Sampling in qualitative interviewing

Sampling in qualitative research has suffered a similar problem to qualitative research in general with the representative random probability samples of quantitative research regarded as the norm to which it should be compared and so found wanting. It is helpful to note Giampietro Gobo's robust view that probability samples are very rarely achieved (or achievable) in social science (Gobo 2007: 405–406). At the risk of repetition, it is odd to talk of a sample or sampling in qualitative social research without a context since whom you research and interview is totally dependent on the nature and design of your study. Some would argue that even the term sample is inappropriate, given that the focus of data generation in qualitative research is on the process rather than an end point of numbers.

In brief, your sample must provide the data you need to produce answers to your research questions, and this process is theory driven in the way described above.

A major characteristic of qualitative research then is that it is theoretically driven, and this also applies to the construction and selection of the sample in a qualitative interview study. The term 'theoretical sampling' was introduced by Barney Glaser and Anselm Strauss (1967) in the context of the development of grounded theory, and over time definitions and practices of both theoretical sampling and grounded theory have been modified by Strauss and others (Corbin and Strauss 2008). Many qualitative researchers use this approach to sampling without necessarily accepting the techniques and strategies advocated by Strauss and colleagues, nor indeed the specific relationship with grounded theory. A more general way of thinking about theoretical sampling in qualitative research is that selection is made on the basis of relevance for your theory, in order to produce a sample that will enable you to develop the theoretical ideas that will be emerging in an iterative process between your theory and your data, and to enable you to test these emerging ideas. This suggests that you will not necessarily start with your sample set in stone, but will modify it and seek further cases in the light of your ongoing analysis of data and the theoretical development emerging from your study. This emerging sample will be both theoretical and purposive, selecting particular exemplary cases for the needs of your study.

One method through which this type of sample can be developed is snowballing, a process in which contact is made with participants appropriate for your research through whatever access route you can find, and through these first participants you are introduced to others of similar/relevant characteristics for your research. This can often be an integral part of ethnography, which involves spending time in the field with the group under study, but is also useful in contacting hard to reach groups and individuals, and perhaps people engaging in criminal or otherwise non-normative or deviant behaviour (Ferrell and Hamm 1998).

In general, academic researchers often favour the convenience sample – available by means of accessibility. Many social science investigations take place on university students, educational practitioners undertake educational research in their own schools and classrooms and people pursue an ethnography on a group of which they are already a part.

The issue of 'how many' interviews, people or cases should be in a qualitative sample is a common question among students hoping to undertake research, and will be discussed in Chapter 6. For now, it is interesting to note the issues around samples and sample size raised in qualitative longitudinal research that takes place through time, typically involving repeat interviews at intervals with the same individuals or groups, because in qualitative longitudinal research many of the considerations of qualitative research in general and interviewing in particular are exacerbated. In relation to sample size, for example, the sample might fall in size due to attrition, or it might grow if, for example, you are following mothers before and after the birth of a child, when the child could join the sample as a toddler (Thomson et al. 2012). Clearly the number of interviews is not the same as the number of cases in this instance. For each member of the sample you will have multiple interviews, and considerably more data than you would have from a one-off, snapshot study. Your procedure for generating a sample will similarly be based on the design, aims and philosophy of your research, but you will need to consider the number of participants with whom you embark on the study, so as not to drown in data and be unable to manage or adequately analyse and interpret the material.

From this discussion, it becomes clear that deciding on an interview sample size, the number of cases appropriate for a given qualitative study is not an easy matter dealt with by some formula, but completely dependent on the nature and design of the study, the aims and research questions and the underlying philosophical position adopted. It is also a characteristic of qualitative research that the sample is built as the research progresses.

The broad social context of qualitative interviews

The broad social context of qualitative research, and so interviews, is multifaceted. The regulations and standards laid down for the conduct of research constitute the research governance regime, which has been growing in coverage and intensity in recent years (discussed further in Chapter 2). Thus, the institution in which the researcher is located will require good practice in research, and an appropriate approach to risk and ethical considerations, particularly in relation to institutional liability. In the personal interaction of the qualitative interview, ethical guidelines (institutional and professional) require no harm to come to participants. The relatively recent emphasis on ethical practice in the social sciences has focused on the researched, with ethical considerations based on protecting them from risk and exploitation and gaining informed consent for the research (see Chapter 6). More recently still there has been concern about the impact of qualitative interviewing on the researcher. Michael Bloor and his colleagues have written extensively about risk and well-being in relation to qualitative researchers drawing out the gendered nature of fieldwork experiences. Women researchers are seen as more vulnerable for example to the emotional demands of fieldwork, and are required to undertake considerable emotional labour and emotion management (Bloor et al. 2007, 2010; Dickson-Swift et al. 2007; Sampson et al. 2008). We discuss emotional issues in interviewing, as well as power in interviews, in Chapter 7.

For the qualitative researcher seeking to undertake interviews for a particular piece of research an important immediate context relates to the social relations of the specific field into which the researcher is about to plunge, with its multiple and often contradictory demands. The interviewer might need to navigate and negotiate in a school, a factory, a large or small organization, a university, a prison (see the discussion on Chapter 4 about where qualitative interviews may be conducted). Access and negotiation might take place with a small social group or network, a group of members of a political movement, or among members of a particular sporting 'tribe'; the list is endless as is the complexity of the social interactions involved.

Conclusion

We have suggested that interviews are ubiquitous in society today, and this is a broad context within which qualitative research using particular types of interview will be taking place. This can be a help and a hindrance. Prospective participants will have ideas about what is expected and required in an interview, which might helpful but might also colour their behaviour in ways that can be a hindrance. It is important for qualitative researchers to be able to draw their participants onto the terrain of the research interview, for them to understand what the research is about, and how the interview will differ from others they might have experienced. We discuss these sorts of practicalities in conducting interviews in Chapter 6.

We have introduced you to qualitative interviews and the terms used to describe them, given an indication of the changing understanding of the relationship between researcher and researched over time, and its connection with the philosophical positions that underpin research, and indicated where these issues are recurrent themes, or will be discussed further in individual chapters in the book. In Chapter 2 we move on to the emergence and history of qualitative interviewing.

2 How have qualitative interviews developed?

Introduction

The systematic use of interviews as a social research method in their own right (rather than part of observation, for example) to explore people's understandings of their lives and aspects of their experiences is relatively recent, from the latter part of the twentieth century. Throughout that time there has been constant interplay between epistemological or philosophical ideas about the nature of social life and our ability to know about it, and how interviews are thought about and practised. Key issues that have woven themselves throughout the history of qualitative interviews are debates about what should be or is the relationship between researchers, the researched and the research. These have manifest themselves in debates about foundations and truth; bias and standardization; reflexivity and construction; and difference and power, among others. Interviews are not, in themselves, inherently biased or unbiased, oppressive or progressive and so on; rather it is the philosophical approach underpinning them that in large part creates such debates.

As well as shifting philosophical stances shaping understandings of the practice of qualitative interviews, the development of research governance procedures and advances in technologies have also played their part in possibilities for and debates about the relationship between researchers, the researched and the research.

Histories of qualitative interviews

Qualitative research, as an acknowledged and systematic approach to knowledge creation, has its roots in the anthropology and sociology of the early decades of the twentieth century (e.g. Malinowski 1922; Mead 1935; Park and Burgess 1925). There are various versions of the history and development of interviews, but Norman Denzin and Yvonne Lincoln's ideas have been especially influential in the qualitative field (2000, 2011). They argue that qualitative social research as a field of enquiry in its own right has operated within eight or nine historical 'moments', from 1900 onwards. We represent these in Table 2.1, which charts a complex field of overlapping phases with legacies that operate simultaneously in the present: 'Successive waves of epistemological theorizing move across these eight moments' (3), from positivist rigour, through interpretive reflexivity, to multiplicity and politicization. Thus qualitative interviewing, encompassed within these broader shifting philosophical phases, aims to achieve and means different things in each of them.

Denzin and Lincoln assert that they are not presenting a progress narrative since all the moments are circulating and competing in the present eighth/ninth moment, but it is difficult not to read their work as a celebration of the emergence of multiple modes of knowing. The moments themselves seem to follow Anthony Giddens' image of a 'runaway world' in late or high modernity (2003) as they speed up during the latter part of the twentieth century and into the first decade of the twenty-first. Perhaps dramatic and constant change appears to us to be the motif of the time period that we are living through, while the past seems to be more stable. Marja Alastalo, for example, points to the 'quite remarkable changes' (2008: 30) that occurred in qualitative methods during the 1920s. The case study method, as qualitative research was usually referred to at the time, came to be regarded as an approach in its own right, often in opposition to the statistical method (though some also saw them as complementary). The idea of 'the case study method' then faded, with the concept of qualitative research and methods emerging post-World War II.

Looking specifically at qualitative interviews and broadly echoing Denzin and Lincoln's depiction of the direction of historical movements entailed in the crisis of representation, Steiner Kvale (1996) refers to a shift in understanding the interview using metaphors of miner or traveller for the interviewer. The miner, or modernist interviewer, is seeking to uncover nuggets of truth through interviews to access a seam of knowledge that is 'out there', ready to be gathered up. The traveller, or postmodern interviewer, embarks upon an interactive and reflective interpretation of how they came to 'see' and transform particular 'sights' into knowledge. Also in line with Denzin, Kvale clearly prefers the postmodern traveller,

Table 2.1 Qualitative research: historical moments (Denzin and Lincoln 2011)

Historical moments	First Traditional	Second Modernist	Third Blurred Genres	Fourth Crisis of Representation	Fifth Postmodern/ Experimental	Sixth Post-Experimental	Seventh Contestation	Eighth/Ninth Now/Future
Time from	1900 →	1950 →	1970 →	1986 →	1990 →	1995 →	2000 →	2010 →
Features	Positivist, foundational paradigm Objectivity Verification	Positivist, foundational paradigm Methodological rigour and procedural formalism Appearance of challenges: post-positivist arguments	Acceptance of post-positivist arguments Emergence of variety of different interpretive perspectives (e.g. feminism, structuralism, cultural studies) and qualitative methods Humanities become central resources Researcher as bricoleur	Change in relations of fieldwork, analysis and writing up Struggle to locate researcher and subjects in texts Reflexive acknowledgement of values, power, social divisions Methodological diaspora – humanists migrate to social sciences, social scientists turn to humanities Text and content blur	Move away from foundational and quasi-foundational Triple crisis of representation, legitimation and praxis Search for evocative, moral critical and local evaluative criteria Experimental creativity using tropes and stories	Composing new ethnographies Literary and rhetorical tropes Narratives and storytelling Autobiography. Multimedia Humanistic social justice	Methodological contestation Backlash from methodological evidence-based social movement Interdisciplinarity Active political and democratic engagement	Moral discourse Sacred textualities Critical conversations about democracy race, gender, class, nation-states, globalization, freedom, community

but acknowledges the presence of the modernist miner operating in the qualitative research interview landscape at the same time.

An alternative view of shifts in the understanding and practice of qualitative interviews is offered by Mike Savage. In the context of a steady growth in qualitative research since the late 1950s/early 1960s in Britain, Savage identifies: 'a distinctive break between what I term "gentlemanly" social science (as a means of making its masculine and bourgeois aspects explicit) which prevailed in 1950, and an emergent professional and "demoralized" social science which was ascending by the mid-1960s' (2010: 12). He makes the case that the 1960s was a period in which the specifically sociological qualitative interview about everyday life was emergent practice in uncharted territory. While researchers had a clear sense of their own importance, there was a lack of clarity in researcher–researched relationships and how they were to treat each other. British social researchers of the early 1960s had not yet come to distinguish their visual observation from the research subjects' elicited narratives in interviews. Observational comments on the interviewees – their appearance, attitudes and behaviour – was regarded as much a means of accessing knowledge as the interviewees' words. This is a process that placed the interviewer as an intellectual and moral authority. In contrast, Savage asserts, contemporary research practice removes the subject as physicality (or at least the researcher's view of it) and turns them into professional text. The means-focused concern of contemporary qualitative researchers with ethical relations between researcher and researched, the avoidance of value judgements about research subjects and prioritizing their voices, has resulted in the researcher hiding their own traces and imprint (Gillies and Edwards 2012).

Conceptions about the place of the researcher in relation to the social world generally, and the people who they interview specifically, vary according to the philosophical approach that they take in conducting their research.

Different philosophical approaches and their understanding of interviews

In what follows, we attempt briefly to introduce a range of philosophical approaches to knowledge that underpin its production, to show how they conceptualize interviews in different ways and consider the implications of this. Our intention is not to offer comprehensive coverage of all possible philosophies that inform social research or detailed accounts of those we do address. Rather, we want to demonstrate that interviews signify different possibilities in relation to the generation of knowledge dependent on the approach. We have loosely followed the convention of shifts in approaches from foundational, through interpretive, to politicization in organizing our discussion, but this in no way implies a developmental progression from one to another. Rather, it is more by way of a mélange of explanations, assertions, links and challenges.

Positivism and interviews

Positivism is not a simple or single concept, and there is no completely shared understanding of the concept. Nonetheless, the main features of positivism are that it distinguishes between the external world and the observer experiencing it, uses observable evidence, and employs objectivity in separating out value-free knowledge gained through systematic procedures from beliefs, feelings and moral stances (Williams 2000). Positivisms' stress on objective reality and truth, as distinct from subjective and varied understandings, means that the production of knowledge is regarded as replicable and thus able to be tried and tested.

What is called a foundational approach is taken to the purpose and process of interviews, where knowledge is deductive, objective and value free. Access to truth and thus to knowledge is through adhering to tried and tested rules of method that are universally applicable, regardless of context. Such an approach may involve standardization, where the researcher ensures that all interviewees are asked the same questions in the same ways. More crucial, however, is the elimination or at the very least minimization of any influence from the researcher, based on concerns that qualitative interviews can lack objectivity and be subject to bias. For accurate data to be obtained in an interview, and in the analysis, researchers need to be impartial and not contaminate an interviewee's report of their activities and experiences. Overall, a positivist approach to interviews demands a mechanistic conception of questions as stimulus and answers as response.

In positivist parlance, the use of interviews is referred to as 'gathering' data because the material is regarded as a report on a reality that is independent of the interviewee. Kvale's metaphor of the interviewer as miner captures this approach to interviewing. Further, because it reflects an independent reality, the data gathered in interviews will be verifiable – interviewees' accounts of behaviour or events being either truthful and reliable, or misleading and distorted. An interviewee's account can be checked for credibility, for example by comparing what he or she says with the researcher's own observations, or official records, or the accounts of other people who were involved in the situation or event (often referred to as triangulation).

An example of positivist claims about knowledge gained through interviewing are those put forward by William Foot Whyte, author of the groundbreaking, classic sociological study *Street Corner Society* (1993), as part of an exchange with postmodern commentators who challenge his work as foundational and positivist-social realist (postmodern approaches are discussed later). Although rejecting the labels of these challenges, in responding to postmodern ideas that there is no distinction between objective, observed knowledge and subjective, inferred phenomena Whyte is asserting key tenets of modernist beliefs rooted in a disinterested observer seeking objective truth with universal validity:

> Physical and social facts can be directly observed or otherwise documented . . . If we accept that [there is no permanent truth only different versions of different stories], we are denying the possibility of building a behavioural science. (1996a: 223, 225)

A direct contrast to this assertion of a distinction between observable fact and subjective meaning and a mechanistic conception of the interview process can be found in interpretive approaches to how the social world works and how people can know about it.

Interpretive approaches and interviews

Interpretivism covers a broad range of different phenomenological philosophical approaches (constructivism, symbolic interactionism, ethnomethodology, etc.) that are all loosely concerned with understanding social phenomena from the perspectives of those involved. Thus in this approach, knowledge takes the form of explanations of how others interpret and make sense of their day-to-day life and interactions (Yanow and Schwartz-Shea 2006).

As human interaction and negotiation is seen as the basis for the creation and understanding of social life in interpretive approaches, it is the interaction of the participants in the interview situation – the researcher and the researched – that creates knowledge. The data in the form of talk that comprises the interview is regarded as a co-construction – what Kvale calls a literal *inter-view*. Kvale's metaphor of the interviewer as traveller gains purchase in these approaches. It does not reach complete fulfilment in many interpretive approaches however because there is still a sense that interviewees can recount and convey to the researcher experiences and feelings that are part of their social world beyond the interview.

An example of knowledge as grasping meaning-making and the interview as co-production is provided in Bill Jordan and colleagues' book *Putting the Family First* (1994). It reports on their study of how parents in higher income households make decisions about participation in the labour market, and they identify the moral project of the book's title as the legitimation that the mothers and fathers drew on in talking about their choices and decisions. In one chapter Jordan and colleagues provide an analysis of the interview interactions that are the basis for their book. They show the interactional order of the 'set piece' of the interview and the presentation of moral and competent selves that it sustains, and how this is most evident when that order is disrupted:

> The research interview is somewhat formal and staid, with an established procedure for taking turns, questions and answer, and polite listening . . . interviewees are invited to tell their stories and are guaranteed a high degree of ritual respect . . . Conversely, there are certain requirements of the research interview that impose constraints. Respondents are supposed to confine themselves to relevant answers and to reply in ways that contribute to the research inquiry (as well as to 'give face' to the interviewer as a serious social scientist) . . . [Some fathers] subverted the interview (and hence their presentation of a morally adequate self) by not giving a coherent, serious account of how what they have made of themselves constituted an instance of putting the family first. Hence the self they achieved in the interview account was heretical in terms of the requirements of individualism and partnership, and risked offending the interviewer and breaching the expectations of the research project. (Jordan et al. 1994: 56, 57)

An example Jordan and colleagues give is of the roles of interviewer (Q) and interviewee (Mr Hazel) momentarily becoming reversed during interaction:

> *Mr Hazel:* I mean would you go and work in the middle of Sheffield or somewhere?
> Q: I've actually got an application in for Sheffield.
> *Mr Hazel:* Why are you going to Sheffield, because it's there I suppose?
> Q: Because it's a job.
> *Mr Hazel:* Because it's a job, absolutely, change your job . . . and if you're young it might be quite a nice and exciting thing, but in terms of people settled with families . . . (1994: 59)

Jordan and colleagues note that it is their male interviewees who are most likely to disrupt the interactional order of the interview. As part of highlighting the unequal gendered nature of social life, feminist approaches also understand knowledge production as deeply gendered.

Feminisms and interviews

There are a number of feminist approaches, including liberal, radical, socialist, standpoint, Black, postmodern, postcolonial and psychoanalytic, but what feminisms largely have in common is a focus on drawing attention to embedded gendered inequalities and power (Tong 2009). Feminist research has often been characterized as *qualitative* research *by* women *on* women and *for* women, but feminists also conduct quantitative research and research on men, and men can conduct research adopting feminist perspectives. Nonetheless, many feminist researchers are concerned with giving voice to women's own accounts of their understandings, experiences and interests, which gives them a strong link to the phenomenological approaches discussed above. In this respect there are arguments not only that a feminist approach has a special affinity with qualitative interviews, but also that feminism has made major contributions to reshaping how qualitative interviewing is understood more broadly (see Doucet and Mauthner 2008 for an excellent discussion).

The second wave of feminist activism and scholarship about the process of qualitative interviews posed a major challenge to male-dominated ideas about the possibility and desirability of a mechanistic, unbiased, scientific, value-free and objective interview. For example, in a now classic, influential piece, Ann Oakley drew on her research on transition to motherhood to contend that detached, uncontaminated interviewing practice was impossible and morally indefensible, and indeed non-hierarchical engagement was a feature of generating knowledge and insight:

> [T]he goal of finding out about people through interviewing is best achieved when the relationship of interviewer and interviewee is non-hierarchical and when the interviewer is prepared to invest his or her own personal identity in the relationship . . . The dilemma of a feminist interviewer interviewing women could be summarised by considering the practical application of some of the strategies recommended in the textbooks for meeting interviewee's questions. For example, these advise that such questions as 'Which hole does the baby come out of?' 'Does an epidural ever paralyse women?' and 'Why is it dangerous to leave a small baby alone in the house?' should be met with such responses from the interviewer as 'I haven't thought enough about it to give a good answer right now', or 'a head-shaking gesture which suggests "that's a hard one"'. (1981: 41)

Oakley raised the idea of reciprocity akin to friendship as a feature of 'women interviewing women'. She suggested that there can be 'no intimacy without reciprocity' (49), where researchers give back something of themselves to their participants.

Oakley's contribution stimulated a rich vein of feminist discussions about the possibilities and impossibilities of non-hierarchical relations, empathy, reciprocity and rapport in qualitative interviewing practice, and the implications for knowledge production. Some have detailed the way that systematic social divisions and characteristics, such as class, ethnicity, age, sexuality and so on, cut across gender and create power imbalances between women researchers and their subjects, and restrict the ability to know the 'Other' through interviews. Others have explored interviews as a two-way flow of power relations between the researcher and the researched, complicating ideas about reciprocity. And still others have questioned the extent to which there is any single, core and coherent social position and identity for both researchers and research subjects within an interview, and any one, coherent knowledge to be constructed (see postmodern approaches later). (See Letherby 2003 for a review of the debates.)

Feminist concerns with giving voice to the marginalized, equality and at least attempting to work with power differentials in interviewing practice and the research process chimes with the idea of emancipatory approaches to interviewing in research with marginalized groups.

Emancipatory approaches and interviews

Key motifs of emancipatory approaches are issues of power and liberation from oppression, and a central tenet is that all people should control their own lives and society generally (e.g. Freire 2006). Traditional or conventional research is regarded as inevitably political since it represents the interests of particular, usually powerful and colonizing, groups in society. The argument is that researchers cannot be independent: they are either on the side of the oppressors or the oppressed. From an emancipatory perspective, the aim of conducting research is to enable the voices of marginalized groups to be heard on their own terms – to understand the world in order to change it and achieve social justice (e.g. Lather 1991).

An emancipatory approach is concerned with the politics of research in fields of life characterized by social discrimination and marginalization, such as minority ethnic and indigenous populations, children and older people, disabled and working-class people. The emphasis is on working collaboratively with, and placing control in the hands of, the people who are living the research topic, rather than researchers. Members of the social group whose lives and circumstances form the subject of the research are viewed as co-constructors of knowledge and validators of claims to knowledge. One way of realizing this is with 'peer' or community researchers: people who live within and have everyday experiences as a member of a particular geographical or social community or social group, and who work alongside academic or professional researchers to generate and understand information collected from their peers for research purposes, including through qualitative interviews (Edwards and Alexander 2011). Another way is through participatory research, where the whole research is controlled by the local or social group in question, rather than by researchers who occupy an advisor role (Cornwall and Jewkes 1995). In this case, it would be the lay researchers who would identify and carry out qualitative interviews as the method that they have selected to help them answer the research questions that they have identified.

Adherents of emancipatory research practice nonetheless identify several tensions and contradictions in the process. The idea of 'better' knowledge being produced through peer and participatory research can be instrumental rather than empowering. Ideas about marginalized group membership can be essentializing and ignore power relations within the group itself. And perhaps most telling, the very activity of pursuing liberation and empowerment through research involves relations of dominance, where emancipation is conferred on disempowered groups by researchers, which runs the risk of perpetuating the status quo.

The dissolution of authoritative, absolute foundations for knowledge in place of marginalized, localized and indigenous understandings can be regarded as one of the hallmarks of liberatory research practice, and in this respect there are links to postmodern approaches.

Postmodernism and interviews

Postmodernism is a broad philosophical term, extending across social science and the arts and humanities. There are several different versions, but postmodern approaches share a turning away from the possibility of universal systems of thought, challenging the legitimacy of meta-narratives, such as modernist beliefs. Dichotomous distinctions between objectivity and subjectivity, fact and fiction, and indeed researcher and researched are regarded as having broken down. There are no straightforward facts and meanings that can form knowledge; rather knowledge and its creation are subject to critique and negotiation, and many versions of the truth exist side by side (O'Donnell 2003).

At their most radical, postmodern approaches detach representation from experience and so challenge the possibility of interviewing (or any other method) as a means of social enquiry, and indeed the endeavour of social research itself. Other postmodernists still see potential and meaning in reflexive interview practice that is aware of the relationship between the means of knowledge production and social reality. As noted in Chapter 1, the postmodern era has been characterized as 'the interview society', in which interviews are central to how people make sense of their lives – the confessional narration is how individual subjectivity is constructed, and how 'internal' experiential truth is understood:

> The interview is part and parcel of our society and culture. It is not just a way of obtaining information about who and what we are; it is now an integral, constitutive feature of our everyday lives. Indeed, as the romantic impulses of interviewing imply, it is at the very heart

> of what we have become and could possibly be as individuals . . . [This implies that] we must think carefully about technical matters because they produce the detailed subject as much as they gather information about him or her. (Gubrium and Holstein 2003a: 29)

Postmodern interviews disrupt the classic technical contours of the designated interviewer – interviewee roles (noted earlier by Jordan et al.); they are not about the imparting of one person's or a group's worldview as interviewees to another who, as researcher, will turn it into knowledge. Interviews cannot refer to some objective reality beyond themselves. Rather, it is the exchange itself, between an interviewee or interviewees and an interviewer, that is of significance and meaning – when, how and why those involved ask questions, construct and tell stories about particular events and experiences in particular ways and so on (see contributions to Gubrium and Holstein 2003b). It is in this approach that Kvale's idea of the researcher as traveller is fulfilled.

Critical realism and interviews

Critical realism assumes the existence of a world that is independent of people's perceptions of it (echoing positivism), but regards that world as accessible only through people's subjectivity and senses, including those of researchers (echoing interpretive approaches). Critical realists are concerned with representing the structural order of the external (material, or material and social) world that underlies the experience of it, and do not regard scientific knowledge as the only means of accessing this order (e.g. Bhaskar 1989).

In terms of qualitative research interviews from a critical realist approach, even if reality and structures are not fully available to people, researchers can still grasp them by working from interviewees' accounts of their understandings and experiences in dialogue with theories about what social reality is like and how it works. The approach also recognizes that researchers' values are inherent in all phases of the research process, and that truth is negotiated through dialogue. Thus, while the objective structuring of reality cannot be comprehended in a perfect way, it can be attempted through the use of qualitative interviewing methods to

> uncover the manifest interactions of the social world, which are then subjected to the transcendental process of theory generation

> to infer the structural conditioning of the interactions . . . [and] to subsequently test the veracity of theories concerning the nature and effects of the structures pertaining. (Porter 2002: 65)

Psychoanalytic approaches and interviews

Psychoanalytic approaches are concerned with emotion and unconscious processes at the heart of subjectivity. They share a commitment to challenging the idea of a rational, knowing subject. Rather, such approaches assume that there are levels of people's perception and experience that are both deeply irrational and difficult to access. Broadly, a psychoanalytic version of subjectivity holds that people resist certain memories, feelings or desires and repress them from conscious thought because they feel them to be bad or forbidden or they do not make sense. People are unconsciously defended against acknowledging and experiencing the ambivalence and anxiety that the internal conflict of feeling things that are deemed unacceptable brings about, through psychic mechanisms such as projection, splitting, transference, fantasy and so on (Elliott 2002).

The implications for conducting qualitative interviews taking a psychoanalytic approach are in the rejection of the idea that people are consciously self-aware and know why they think, say and do, and can report this directly to researchers (as with interpretive approaches). Researchers taking a psychoanalytic approach to interviews thus argue for the use of an unstructured narrative mode to allow room for unconscious processes to surface (a hidden psychic structuring that has some echoes of the critical realist structuring of reality), as well as multiple and inconsistent subjectivity (with resonances with postmodern understandings of personhood and knowledge). The seven aspects of enabling knowing through the psychoanalytic research interview that Kvale (1996) identifies, for example, include: the intensive individual case study; the open and non-directive mode of interviewing; the interpretation of meaning that allows for ambiguity and contradiction; the temporal dimension intertwining past, present and future; and human interaction involving emotions.

Valerie Walkerdine and colleagues (2002) report role disruption behaviour on the part of some of their male interviewees similar to that identified by Jordan et al. earlier, but have a different reading of its meaning from a psychoanalytic perspective: that these men were defending themselves from feelings of vulnerability stirred up by the interview (191). Interest in unconscious processes is not centred on those of the interviewee alone, however; the subjectivity of the researcher is also implicated. The detached interviewer of positivist approaches, in this model, is a defended researcher:

> What is being defended against are intrusive feelings about the research process, the subjects and the relationship between the two ... It is therefore crucial to acknowledge and attempt to understand what transferences and counter transferences might be telling us as researchers. (Walkerdine et al. 2002: 186)

While researchers use different philosophical frameworks to understand the production of knowledge through social research, and think through the implications of conducting qualitative interviews, they do so within the context of other – more prosaic and institutional – parameters that govern the research process.

What does the institution of research governance procedures mean for how we think about interviews?

Research governance is a term covering a range of regulations, principles and standards that lay down what is considered good practice in research. The governance regime addresses issues such as risk assessment, health and safety, ethical conduct and so on. The institutionalization of social research regulation is often traced back to instances of bad practice in clinical research (such as taking and storing organs from dead babies without parental consent), from where the perceived need for governance expanded into social research, along with the general rise of an 'audit culture'. Research governance is said to safeguard research participants' interests and rights, protect researchers from allegations of bad practice by providing a clear framework for them to work within and promote and enhance research quality. Systems of research governance have the merit of ensuring that researchers undertake a full and reflexive consideration of the process of conducting research, thinking through the implications of their plans and practice.

Nonetheless, many qualitative researchers have been vocal in laying out what they regard as a highly bureaucratized and damaging ethics regulatory regime creep (e.g. see contributions to a debate section in *Sociological Research Online*, 2010, http://socresonline.org.uk/15/4). The requirement for researchers to detail a range of aspects of their research process and gain approval from a regulatory body (whether university or other institutional base) has implications for the conduct of qualitative research interviews, especially for researchers who wish to conduct interviews within emancipatory/participatory or psychoanalytic approaches. The need to (a) detail what the research is about and the tools that will be used, and (b) provide written information sheets to research subjects and gain their written informed consent to participate, prior to conducting the research in order to gain approval to proceed, cuts across participant-led agendas and attempts to equalize research relationships. It does not sit well with the elicitation of free narratives that is the aim of psychoanalytic research interviews. Further, there is a risk that asking questions about certain, 'sensitive' subjects may be ruled out of interviews in advance by regulatory bodies, whether or not research participants want to talk about the issue. It is a moot question as to whether some of the classic social research studies, such as Whyte's study of status in gangs in the slums of Boston (*Street Corner Society*, discussed earlier), would have gained ethical approval under the current research governance regime.

What do advances in technology mean for how we practice and think about interviews?

Available technologies have long shaped the practice of qualitative interviews. Prior to the development in the 1950s of portable audio tape-recorders, now followed by even lighter and smaller digital recorders, researchers conducting interviews relied on memory. Whyte carried out the fieldwork for *Street Corner Society* (1993) in the 1930s, on which he remarks:

> With my informants, I had to rely on memory. At first, I could recall very little. As I wrote my notes, I found that I was remembering more and more as time went on. I cannot claim that my notes are a verbatim report of all that had been said – and in the particular order and sequence. Nevertheless, when the informant made a strong positive or negative statement about somebody or

> something, I could be almost positive that I had those exact words. (1996b: 243)

Les Back (2010) provides an interesting assessment of the strengths and limitations of the tape recorder as the primary tool of qualitative research, stimulated by the 'death' of his own device. As part of this he ponders whether or not a recording tool that captures participants' spoken words verbatim confines the researcher through confusing socially shaped accounts with authentic truth (discussed further in Chapter 6). The technology of computer-mediated communication also reshapes the practice of interviewing and understanding the nature of interviews. Online interviewing, either synchronously or asynchronously, in public or private arenas, enables the transcendence of boundaries of time and space, reaching beyond the constraints of face-to-face contact. But there are concerns about the way that interviewing online can cut across the socio-emotional signals between researchers and subjects that take place in face-to-face interactions, about the 'truth' of identity and authenticity of experience claims, about the flows and bases of power, as well as the challenges for research governance and ethics (Hine 2001; James and Busher 2006). Clearly these concerns will have quite different implications within each of the various philosophical approaches discussed here. We follow up the process of online interviewing in Chapter 5.

The development and widespread availability of computer-aided qualitative data analysis software (CAQDAS) that facilitates the analysis of transcribed qualitative interview texts, as well as graphics, audio and visual material, has generated discussions about its usefulness and implications (e.g. Séror 2005). In the context of our discussion here, this includes some tensions about what CAQDAS means for conceptions of the nature of interviews as they become 'fixed' as fact in electronic files, existing as a reality outside of the context of their production, potentially available as an independent product to the interaction and people that produced them. To what extent is it inherent in these technological advances – as Natasha Mauthner and Odette Parry have discussed in relation to qualitative interview data preservation and sharing through archives – that the foundational assumptions of modernism are reproduced, or at least in part form the implicit philosophical terms in which researchers practising qualitative interviews engage with such technologies?:

> [W]hat Bourdieu terms 'epistemic reflexivity' goes beyond the individual scholar and takes as its focus on analysis 'scientific practice', modes of knowledge production, and the 'epistemological unconscious' underpinning these. (Mauthner and Parry, 2009: 301)

In the chapters that follow, we go on to explore and reflect on the forms, settings, tools and practices of the interview mode of knowledge production.

3 What forms can qualitative interviews take?

Introduction

In this chapter we discuss the various forms of interviews including ethnographic, oral history, life course, life history, biographical, narrative interviews, as well as group interviews. Throughout our discussion, we link them to the broad philosophical positions underlying their use. Other modes of interviewing and ways of combining these types of interviews with other methods, qualitative and quantitative, are also considered.

General forms of qualitative interviews

The major forms of qualitative interviews are semi- and unstructured interviews. In a typical semi-structured interview the researcher has a list of questions or series of topics they want to cover in the interview, an interview guide (see Chapter 5 for examples), but there is flexibility in how and when the questions are put and how the interviewee can respond. The interviewer can probe answers, pursuing a line of discussion opened up by the interviewee, and a dialogue can ensue. In general the interviewer is interested in the context and content of the interview, how the interviewee understands the topic(s) under discussion and what they want to convey to the interviewer. Basically these interviews allow much more space for interviewees to answer on their own terms than structured interviews, but do provide some structure for comparison across interviewees in a study by covering the same topics, even in some instances using the same questions. For example, in a study of young women's sexuality one of us has employed a topic guide and a naturalistic interview, but needed to ask a few questions about the young women's basic knowledge of HIV/AIDS (Holland et al. 2004). These questions were asked in the same format of all (147) participants, at a point in the interview that the researcher involved considered appropriate.

In the unstructured interview the researcher clearly has aims for the research and a topic of study, but the importance of the method is to allow the interviewee to talk from their own perspective using their own frame of reference and ideas and meanings that are familiar to them. Flexibility is the key with the researcher able to respond to the interviewee, to trace the meaning that s/he attaches to the 'conversation with a purpose' (Burgess 1984: 102), to develop unexpected themes and adjust the content of interviews and possibly the emphasis of the research as a result of issues that emerge in any interview. The researcher can have an *aide memoire* to remind them of areas into which to lead the conversation (see Chapter 5). Or they can use a single question to begin the interview, where the interviewee is prompted to embark on their story. The latter can be the case in some psychological or psychosocially oriented interviews and in some oral history or biographical approaches. Flexibility is key to the unstructured interview and phenomenological philosophical approaches underlie the method – constructivism, symbolic interactionism and ethnomethodology.

Both semi- and unstructured interviews are qualitative methods in use across the social sciences. The form of the interview might be similar, or even the same; what will differ are the particular theoretical positions and concomitant approaches to analysis and interpretation adopted by the researcher from their philosophical and possibly also their disciplinary perspective.

Specific forms of qualitative interviews

The ethnographic interview

Ethnography is historically the basic qualitative method deriving from early twentieth-century anthropology, although now widely used in many other social science disciplines. Ethnography is itself constructed from multiple qualitative methods, including observation and participant observation, and can incorporate the collection of demographic and other statistical data about the researched as appropriate (see discussion of mixed methods later). Critically, however, ethnography involves social exploration, *protracted investigation*, spending time in the field, the site of study, and the interpretation of local and situated cultures based on paying attention to the singular and concrete (Atkinson and Hammersley 1994; Atkinson et al.

2001). In the anthropological model people go off and spend a long time in the field with their chosen group. Interviews are clearly important, initially perhaps with a key informant who can provide crucial information about the individuals, groups and social relations within the chosen research setting. Key informants have a formal or informal position that gives them specialist knowledge about the people and processes that are the subject of research (such as preacher, head of department, oldest club member). Interviews with key informants can help illuminate situations, behaviours and attitudes that researchers otherwise could not access or understand. But equally key informants can mislead the researcher or withhold knowledge in interviews. For example, arguably 'Doc', the leader of one of the gangs who was William Foot Whyte's key informant for his *Street Corner Society* ethnography (see Chapter 2), steered Whyte's understanding and interpretation of people and situations.

Interviews in the field can be formal (perhaps recorded, perhaps using an interview guide) or informal, on the hoof, as and when an appropriate situation, person or group becomes available. In this instance flexibility, practice in recall and making notes after the event become key researcher/ interviewing skills. It is possible to use a small unobtrusive audio recorder in some informal settings, depending on the relationship with the participants and the types of setting. Shane Blackman undertook an ethnography investigating youth cultures, including following groups of young people into a range of settings using a tape recorder. One of his groups, New Wave Girls, made a tape for him:

> We made this tape the other night. We thought you would like it because you're studying us and doing tapes. So we did one for you. Can we have it back sometime; we thought we'd help you, suppose. You coming for the walk?

Blackman reports that these girls were already heavily involved in documenting personal and group history, and throughout the fieldwork he collected letters, poems and pictures from them. He saw the tape as an attempt to influence the collection of data on themselves. And indeed it was successful, its analysis forming a chapter in his book (Blackman 1995).

More recently 'ethnographic interview' has been used in a way akin to 'qualitative, unstructured interview' particularly in its spread to disciplines other than anthropology, and given the time and economic constraints on protracted periods of research immersion. In a history of the development of ethnographic interviews, Barbara Sherman Heyl emphasizes 'the time factor – duration and frequency of contact – and the quality of the emerging relationship' (2001: 368). But she also identifies key features of the ethnographic interview as aiming to empower interviewees to shape the questions being asked, and possibly the focus of the research, according to their own worldviews and meanings, and reflexivity. In this regard she is drawing on interpretivist and feminist understanding of the interview. In the past the ethnographer had been regarded as an aloof, objective seeker after knowledge, whose writing up of the research provided an authoritative authorial voice. The textual turn in ethnography in the 1980s and the emphasis on reflexivity in research from feminists and others were key to the overthrow of this idea, and the qualitative researcher was recognized as historically positioned, locally situated and the very human observer/participant we can see in the changes sketched in the chapters of this book.

A yet more recent development has been that of autoethnography, based on postmodern philosophy, where the researcher her- or himself is the subject/object of the research and reflexivity is at its core. Autoethnographies 'are highly personalized accounts that draw upon the experience of the author/researcher for the purposes of extending sociological understanding' (Sparkes 2000: 21). Sarah Wall writes an informative and engaging autoethnography of her attempt to understand what it is – 'Despite their wide-ranging characteristics, autoethnographic writings all begin with the researcher's use of the subjective self' (2006: 8) – how to do it, and criticisms of the method. These include self-indulgence, narcissism, introspection and lack of rigour (Atkinson 1997; Coffey 1999). Wall concludes that pursued with rigour the method can contribute to knowledge. (See too Jones 2005.)

Eliciting the interviewee's own story

One set of forms of interviews are specifically designed to elicit a story, their own story from the participants in the research, with particular inflections from the originating stance of the research. These are oral history, life course, life history, biographical and narrative interviews.

Oral history draws its methods from history and sociology and emphasizes the importance of time and memory, and people are interviewed about their past experiences. Oral historians also tend to try to give expression to marginalized voices, particularly in relation to class, gender and ethnicity (Bornat 2012). Paul Thompson makes a distinction between oral history, which for him is focused on the past, and life history, which is focused on the present and can cover the whole life (Thompson 2008: 19, 1975; Thompson et al. 1983). From this perspective in oral history approaches the focus of enquiry and the question(s) facilitating talk in the interview could relate to the interviewee's life experiences of a particular historical event or period, for example, World War II, the millennium, or to a particular biographical life event. This event could be their earliest memory, or the birth of their first child, for example. In life history the focus and facilitating question(s) could be more wide ranging, covering various aspects of their life (work, family, home). The question(s) could open up the possibility of the interviewee telling their whole life story in their own words. In some versions of this approach the aim is to elicit this story, which could be seen as an autobiography, with the researcher staying very much out of the picture after the initial question or prompt (see later). In each of these types of interview, points can be followed up with supplementary questions if necessary, or to clarify the meaning of what is being said if there is any doubt, and both versions can be combined with other sources of data such as documents – diaries, photographs, letters and so on (see Chapter 5).

Bringing the *life course* into consideration in these biographical approaches draws attention to normative expectations that can constrain or enable individuals at particular stages of life, the effects of biological ageing and cohort effects of being members of a particular generation. For example, in the United Kingdom the generation who experienced the deprivations of the 1930s and World War II were followed by the post-1945 baby boomers, who have come under attack in the current constrained economic climate for being the 'having it all' generation, leaving a more sparse life for the generations who now follow them (see Edwards et al. 2014). All of these elements, normative expectations, biological ageing and cohort effects will interact, affecting the individual life as both lived and told, and could be the focus of attention, or at least consideration, in designing a study using life history and biographical methods. They can also play a part in analysis, interpretation and understanding.

The *life history* method was pioneered by W. I. Thomas and Florian Znaniecki, and exemplified by an autobiography written for them by a

Polish peasant Wladek Wisznienski – the first to be used as sociological data. In their view the individual case can give access to the social:

> In analysing the experiences and attitudes of an individual we always reach data and elementary facts which are not exclusively limited to this individual's personality but can be treated as mere instances of more or less general classes of data or facts, and thus be used for the determination of laws of social becoming. (Thomas and Znaniecki 1958: II 1832)

Overall in their monumental work they used letters and other 'life records' of Polish immigrants to access the story and history of Polish immigration to the United States, their concern being to draw subjective aspects of experience into an understanding of the social (Thomas and Znaniecki 1958). Although 'life history' and 'life story' are sometimes used interchangeably, Robert Miller (2000: 19) suggests that in the history of the method, an early distinction was made between life story as an account of their life given by one individual, and life history where other sources, including newspaper reports and public records, could validate the individual account. This confirmation or validation through external sources (triangulation) can be seen as related to the statistical modes of social enquiry which swept into a dominant position in sociology in the 1950s. In this period qualitative and biographical methods became relatively submerged.

A resurgence ensued in the 1970s, however, drawing on the influential work of C. Wright Mills who was concerned with the interplay between personal biography, history and society, and argued that 'neither the life of an individual nor the history of a society can be understood without understanding both' (Mills 1959: 3). Prue Chamberlayne and colleagues have suggested that these methods have become more popular among social scientists in recent years, which they describe as a turn to biographical methods. In this period, an interview that pursues aspects of an individual's biography has become used more widely in the social sciences (Chamberlayne et al. 2000). In most cases one aspect of the biography might be sought, for example, experience of childbirth, of family life, of health or perhaps educational or career trajectories. The focus might be quite tight, for example, experiences of a particular type of educational scheme or institution. Whatever the topic of the research the principles of the interview will be the same and depend on the underlying approach, but the practice might vary.

One particular type of *biographical interview* is employed in the Biographic-Narrative Interpretive Method (BNIM) (Chamberlayne et al. 2000; Wengraf 2001). Here a single question is aimed to induce a non-interrupted narrative from the interviewee, with the interviewer making as little intrusion as possible into the story. The researchers who developed this method take a phenomenological approach to understanding biographical data, focusing on the individual's perspective within a knowable historical and structural context, that is, some external (historical/social) facts of their life can be known (Bornat 2008). They have developed a specific analytic process for this type of interview, although other types of narrative analysis could also be used (Rosenthal 2004; Wengraf with Chamberlayne 2006).

From an interpretivist perspective, the *narrative interview* is based on the idea that people produce narratives about the self and identity through time that draw not only on their own experiences and understanding, but on culturally circulating stories that help them interpret and make sense of the world and themselves in it: 'They are interpretive devices through which people represent themselves, both to themselves and to others' (Lawler 2002: 246). Riessman (1993) provides a thorough introduction to narrative research and analysis with many examples, and also draws attention to performative aspects of the narratives produced by participants:

> Personal narratives contain many performative features that enable the 'local achievement of identity' (Cussins 1998). Tellers intensify words and phrases, they enhance segments with narrative detail, reported speech, appeals to the audience, paralinguistic features ('uhms') and gestures, or body movement. (Riessman 2001: 701)

Others similarly regard the relationship between life and narratives as crucial for self-identity – Giddens highlights the importance of maintaining the continuity of self-identity in the everyday world, which he sees as the capacity to 'keep a particular narrative going' (1991: 4). We might produce a relatively stable and coherent self through the narrative we produce, but to do so we need to have an idea of our past, present and possible futures, although these ideas might be contingent and unstable. This will require us to work and rework the past in revisiting and recounting our memories in relation to the changing present and potential futures. Qualitative longitudinal researchers can have direct experience of this subsequent overwriting of the past when returning to interviewees after a period of time has elapsed. In different types of interviews these narratives might be fragmented and partial, but they will always provide a link to the social positioning and experience of the storyteller in the social and historical context.

All of the approaches discussed here can be seen as eliciting a narrative from the interviewee, and the particular choice of interview type will relate to the aims and underlying framework of the research as delineated here, although in the literature there can be some blurring of terms. The participation of the researcher can also vary. S/he can stand apart, encouraging the interviewee to tell their story uninterrupted as in the BNIM method; s/he can share aspects of their own narrative with the interviewee, particularly if the specific research topic is about a shared experience, for example, being overseas postgraduate students in the United Kingdom (Gill and Goodson 2011). In this case the researcher shared her story with the participant and they had follow up conversations to collaborate on filling gaps in the narratives of each. The final step after drafting a narrative sketch involved participant and researcher locating individual stories in their wider historical context and social and cultural practices (162). So over time the approach in this study led to the third position where the researcher regards herself and the participant as co-producers of the narrative. All of the forms of interviews discussed here understand the interview as giving some level or kind of access to the social/historical as well as to the individual.

We have largely been talking about individual interviews so far, but the group interview is also an important route into participant's social worlds, particularly for illuminating group dynamics.

Focus group interviews

The term group interview can be used generically to describe any interview in which a group of people take part, but can be differentiated from the focus group interview. Many definitions of focus groups exist in the literature, but essentially they involve a small group of people engaging in collective discussion of a topic previously selected by the researcher. With their origins in market research, as a research technique in social science focus groups have elicited a range of criticisms, and gone in and out of fashion (Merton 1987; Morgan 1997; Morgan and Spanish 1984). Among advocates, appropriate group numbers can range widely and will depend on the nature of the study and the specific situation of the group, but six to ten is often suggested in the literature. Many groups reported have perforce been smaller. Particular emphasis has been placed on the interaction that takes place between the participants, the group dynamics, and the insight and data that this can produce (Kitzinger 1994, 1995). Typically the researcher moderates, or runs the discussion, with a series of questions to guide its course. But a stimulus can provide a focus or starting point, for example, a photograph, film, vignette or game. If resources allow, a second researcher can be present making notes on the interactions, and identifying speakers as an aid to transcription and recognition of the participant in the recording. The use of video is associated with the topic and the underlying approach of the research, for example, video-recording children's interactions in the primary school.

The construction of focus groups is guided by the topic of research and research questions. They could be, for example, people at the same, or different, levels in the organization under study; people of the same age, class, gender; people of varying ages, classes and genders depending on the issue under study; naturally occurring groups – for example, occupational, or members of specific groups as in a rowing club. So members of the group might know each other, as in the latter, or know some or none of the group as in Janet Smithson's (2000) groups who were single-sex groups of people at similar life stages, that is, university students, in vocational training, young unemployed, in semi-skilled or professional jobs. Smithson draws attention to the public performance aspects of the groups and the moderator's constraints and guidance, particularly for consideration in analysis and interpretation. She also suggests that analysis should see accounts that are produced in different contexts as products of those contexts. These contexts include the micro-geographies of socio-spatial relations and meanings of space and place, discussed in Chapter 4.

Focus groups can be used alone, or in conjunction with other methods, and often individual and focus group interviews are used. Focus groups can be used at the start of a project, for generating ideas about the participants under research, since their interaction can give insight into participants' worldview, the language they use and their values and beliefs about a particular issue or topic, useful in design of the study. They can be used at the end, to get feedback on results or for assessment in an evaluation design. The rapidity with which data can be generated in focus (and other) groups is valued, but the logistical and practical issues of organizing focus groups should not be overlooked, even when the participants might all be in one organization or location. See too Kate Stewart and Matthew Williams (2005) for a consideration of undertaking focus groups online.

Focus group interviews might be seen as more appropriate for non-sensitive, low-involvement topics, but many argue for their value in just such contexts, and they have been widely used, for example, in studying sexuality. Hannah Frith (2000) highlights some advantages provided by focus groups in this field. They can provide conditions in which people feel comfortable discussing sexual experiences, particularly shared experiences. Agreement between group members can help to build an elaborated picture of their views; disagreement may lead to participants defending their views and provide further explanation. Others illustrate their value in studies on violence against women and corruption in Tanzania (Jakobson 2012), and young women who have been victims of sexual abuse in Sweden (Overlien et al. 2005). Lori Peek and Alice Fothergill (2009) argue that focus groups can serve a social support or empowerment function, and illustrate the strength of the method used with marginalized, stigmatized or vulnerable participants. Pitching their discussion at a more general level, George Kamberelis and Greg Dimitriadis (2005) review the history of focus groups, in particular in relation to pedagogy, politics and social enquiry, arguing that critical focus groups in these areas (and their articulation) in empowering participants can create the conditions for the emergence of a critical consciousness directed towards social change.

Focus group interviews can then be a useful method in a range of contexts. As ever, the decision to use the method is dependent on its appropriateness for the particular piece of research, its theoretical and philosophical approach and the research questions.

Couple interviews

We have suggested that the focus group is particularly valuable in giving access to social interaction, and a further type of interview offers access to a very particular type of interaction – between couples. The general form of this joint interview is when one researcher interviews two participants who usually know each other. This can happen when the interviewee asks for another person to be present, or perhaps someone in the setting intrudes upon the interview and stays (a parent when a child is being interviewed, a husband when a wife is the main interviewee). It can also be appropriate in studies of illness and disability, in this case involving a carer and the care recipient. The more specific version is in a planned design and involves two people who are in a couple relationship, for example, husband and wife, heterosexual or same-sex partners (Bjornhold and Regland 2012; Doucet 1996; Duncombe and Marsden 1993; Heaphy and Einarsdottir 2012; Weeks et al. 2001), as we describe for Doucet's household portrait technique in Chapter 5. The design often involves both couple interviews and individual interviews with the partners separately and can take place in the context of a family study, where children are also interviewed, with or without parent(s) (Backett 1990; Harden et al. 2010; Valentine 1999).

Margunn Bjornholt and Gunhild Farstad enter what they describe as a methodological controversy about 'whether couples should ideally be interviewed together or apart' (2012: 1) stressing the strengths of joint couple interviews. In their work on gender, work and care they found that the advantages included: solving the ethical problems of anonymity and consent among interviewees where people know each other; providing a 'common reflective space' (15) with corroborations, extensions and disagreements contributing to rich data; providing observation opportunities of behaviour and interaction; and practical advantages in organizing the interviews. They suggest that 'joint interviews with interviewees who share some kind of personal relationship should be recognized as a separate form of the qualitative research interview' (15). Brian Heaphy and Anna Einarsdottir who interviewed couples in civil partnerships both together and apart point out that the 'narratives are the product of the situated interactional context in which they emerge, and involve the negotiation of agency and constraint: put another way, they involve complex flows of power' (2012: 15). The context (and audience) includes the researcher, the partner, broader audiences for the research and the socio-cultural context. In their work the joint interviews produced couple and marriage stories and the individual interviews produced biographically embedded narratives of relating selves. The latter complicated and contextualized the couple stories, and enabled the researchers to make links between the relational scripts that were produced in interviews and flows of power in relational and socio-cultural contexts. Heaphy and Einarsdottir suggest that in the light of changing relational possibilities, including civil partnerships and gay marriage, but also more generally an interactionist methodology based on joint and individual interviews orientated towards narrative analysis is an appropriate research strategy for exploring the complexities of relational realities.

Mixing qualitative interviewing with other methods

The most usual mixing referred to in the context of social research is the mixing of quantitative and qualitative methods, and we can see from our earlier discussions that this could raise issues about incompatibility of the underpinning philosophy and epistemology of these approaches. These issues have indeed provided the basis for continuing debate, rejection and/or support for mixing methods over many years, with heightened interest in recent decades with the growth and rapid expansion of the mixed methods field (Brannen 1992; Johnson et al. 2007; Teddlie and Tashakkori 2010). Julia Brannen (2005) has suggested, like Alan Bryman (1988), that pragmatic or technical rather than philosophical assumptions drive much research in practice, and even when researchers plan to choose methods in line with the framing of a particular research question and its philosophical assumptions, in practice this might not occur. Jennifer Mason (2006: 9) argues for the importance of a qualitatively informed logic of explanation for theoretically driven mixed-methods research. She suggests that qualitative thinking is a useful starting point for thinking outside the box, and ultimately her preferred approach involves multi-dimensional research strategies that transcend or subvert the qualitative–quantitative divide.

But it is also possible to mix methods within qualitative and quantitative approaches (Williams and Vogt 2011). As we have seen, qualitative studies very often combine several qualitative methods, and ethnography is a typical case in this regard. This mixing can involve qualitative interviews with other types of qualitative methods, life history or different versions of narrative interviews combined with documentary analysis, for example. Different types of interviews can be used in the same study, individual interviews combined with focus groups, face-to-face with telephone or email interviews, and all combined with different types of documentary and archival data.

In mixing across paradigms, there is considerable discussion about which takes priority, qualitative or quantitative, and models have been developed with one or the other prioritized (Brannen 2005). Others argue for qualitative and quantitative data to be given equal weight in a study. Jo Moran-Ellis and colleagues (2006, 2007; Cronin et al. 2008) provide an example of mixing methods across paradigms, using quantitative data, and multiple qualitative methods (different types of interviews) in five small studies exploring the understandings, experiences and management of everyday vulnerability in the lives of a wide range of people living in 'Hilltown'. The studies were methodologically linked but discrete in terms of data. Vulnerability could occur at the area level (statistics on risk of crime, flooding, etc.), the spatial environment, the community, the household and the individual. The researchers' objective was to integrate the methods, arguing that this approach gives equal weight to the contribution of different methods in understanding the phenomenon under study, each data set contributing to answering the research question in their own paradigmatic terms. They also mixed within paradigm, in using different types of qualitative interviews in four of the studies. These produced visual data through photo-elicitation and video interviews focused on neighbourhood; narrative data from in-depth interviews with homeless participants; household interviews, including individual interviews with all household members, which could be aggregated to the household level; and individual in-depth interviews with participants who lived alone. They developed a model to accomplish integration at the level of analysis, 'following the thread', e.g. of 'physical safety', through each dataset.

Sheila Henderson and colleagues (2007) used focus group and individual depth interviews in the first phase of a qualitative longitudinal study of young people's values and transitions (McGrellis et al. 2000). They also employed a survey of youth values (1,800 young people), using some questions as in the European Values Survey (Ashford and Timms 1992), to compare their views with adults, provide background information about youth values and material on young people's concerns to draw on in designing the subsequent focus groups (62), which in turn contributed to the content of depth interviews (57) with selected young people. The different elements were integrated at the level of research design and, as with Moran and colleagues, equal weight given to each element. They were initially analysed separately, each contributing to specific research questions pursued in the research, and then integrated in analyses related to other research questions (Henderson et al. 2007).

Conclusion

In this chapter we have detailed forms of specific qualitative interviews that elicit narratives, biographies, life stories and histories from participants, linking them to their philosophical grounding. We have discussed the qualitative interview in the context of mixing methods. In the following chapter we build on this discussion of types of interviews to consider the different contexts in which any of them might occur, with particular reference to space and place.

4 Where can qualitative interviews take place?

Introduction

In Chapter 3 we discussed forms that the qualitative interview can take. Here we discuss further types of interview, focusing on and considering the implications of the setting for the type of interaction that takes place and the data that can be generated. We examine the importance of various settings for face-to-face interviews, and variants of 'walking and talking' interviews. The discussion continues with interviews where the researcher and researched are in different places: self-interviews where the researcher is not present, telephone, online and e-interviews in cyberspace, where the researched and researcher can be still further apart, although in some instances in visual contact.

Interview settings

Earlier we have discussed pragmatic approaches to issues of research methodology and method, and a pragmatic approach to the location of face-to-face interviews (as might be advocated in text books) would suggest finding a space that is available for use, convenient and accessible to participant and researcher, where you could avoid interruption and make an adequate sound recording of the conversation. Any experienced researcher will smile at this point, thinking of the places and spaces in which they have undertaken interviews, some of which probably met none of these criteria. Privacy might be an issue and so a private rather than a public space is more suitable, the home of researcher or researched possibly, each bringing their own concerns and complications. But private rooms can be available in otherwise public spaces, the researcher's office in a university, or the office of the participant in an organization of which they are part. We can see that just naming these potential settings for an interview further complicates an already complex situation in relation to the power and positionality (their social status and identity) of the researcher and researched in a range of hierarchies. (See also Chapter 7.)

Positions in hierarchies of gender, class, age, ethnicity and other dimensions are not just aspects of the multiple identities of individuals (or groups) but are experienced, created and enacted in *places*. Think of a school, redolent of power hierarchies; a researcher accessing children in school has multiple levels of power and control to negotiate, and once in contact with the children the adult–child power relationship itself colours the interaction. It is hard for a child or young person interviewed in a school setting not to see the researcher as a teacher, or allied with teachers/adults in this context. On their part teachers and other powerful figures can undermine the confidentiality offered to children, expecting access to any information gathered. But homes too have their own micro geographies and sets of familial power relations, and spaces in homes available for research vary considerably with the social positioning of the participants. It can be argued that the public permeates the private, and the domestic space is increasingly linked to public space through media and the internet in an increasingly two-way process with the growth of social media.

Micro-geographies of interview sites

Often researchers offer the choice of setting to the interviewee, who might like to meet in a public place in which they are comfortable – a café, a pub, a park. Noise affecting the recording, being able to hear what each other says adequately, and privacy are practical considerations here. These can also apply to workplaces of different types: factories, a prison, an open plan office, a school staff room. If other people are within hearing distance, or can enter the space where the interview takes place, this can create tension for both interviewer and interviewee and affect how and what can be discussed. When undertaking research in different institutions and organizations, the researcher may be facilitated by the provision of a suitable room, or left to take their chances in whatever spaces are available.

Aspects of identity can be experienced and enacted in particular spaces and places, but they can also be evoked, affecting the way in which participants respond. Interviewing neighbourhood organization staff and residents about their experiences of, actions in and perceptions of their neighbourhood, Sarah Elwood and Deborah Martin (2000) found different kinds of answers given, depending on where the interview was conducted. For example, community organization directors and staff when interviewed in their offices tended to give explanations based primarily on the priorities of the organization. Interviewed in other public places or in their homes, they tended to talk more freely about their own opinions separate from organizational goals, giving examples drawn from their experiences of the neighbourhood through other aspects of their identities, for example, volunteering at local schools, relationships with neighbours.

In general these researchers suggest that the interview site itself produces 'micro-geographies' of socio-spatial relations and meaning that reflect the relationships of the researcher with the participant, the participant with the site and the site within a broader socio-cultural and power context that affects both researcher and participant (Elwood and Martin 2000: 649, 650). They advocate that much greater attention should be paid to interview sites, pointing to the importance they have for the research at every level, from research plan and questions, through generation of data, understanding power relations between researcher and researched and gaining insight into the basic questions under study.

At the pragmatic level, as researchers we do desire a room where we can speak privately to the research participant(s). Many researchers have also pointed out that the interview site, in all its messiness and social embeddedness, is a source of information and data beyond that generated in the interview. Seeing the participant in context (in their home, their classroom, their workplace), surrounded by the material culture of their created space, and possibly interacting with others in that space, offers a wealth of information beyond that obtained, and possibly obtainable, in an interview, providing an ethnographic dimension to the exchange.

A further type of interview builds on the access that space and place can provide researchers to the lives, identities, biographies and memories of participants. The walking interview takes place in the participant's environment.

Walking and talking

As with many methods and types of qualitative interview, the walking interview has its roots in ethnography and is not new. Margarethe Kusenbach (2003: 463) describes the 'go-along' method as both more limited and more focused than the generic ethnographic practice of 'hanging out'. In this version participants are accompanied on a 'natural' outing, rooted in everyday routines with the researcher asking questions, listening and observing, exploring the participant's practices and experiences as they move through and interact with their physical and social environment. The go-alongs can be accomplished on foot or in a vehicle. In Kusenbach's study they could last from a few minutes to an entire day, but she suggests 90 minutes as a productive length of time. They provide insight into perception, spatial practices, personal biographies, the web of connections between people and patterns of social interaction.

Andrew Clark and Nick Emmel (2010) provide useful advice about undertaking walking interviews, outlining some of the advantages. Placing events, stories and experiences in their spatial context can help participants to articulate their thoughts; the narratives can add detail to the researcher's understanding and insight; and locations can be used to elicit or prompt discussion, encouraging questioning that might not occur in a room setting. The researchers provided information and a digital camera, and discussed the rationale before the walk so that participants knew what was expected, pointing out that guidance needs to be clear enough to ensure that appropriate data are obtained, but sufficiently open to let participants present their neighbourhood (2). The participants chose the route. The interview was digitally recorded, using a good quality small microphone with a wind guard. The researchers later recorded the route on a map and wrote it onto the transcript of the interview, with annotations on what was being discussed and where photos were taken (see Figure 4.1). People met en route will be seen with the researcher on their own patch and so confidentiality is threatened, and others who join the conversation need to be told that it is being recorded.

With impetus from geographers and the 'new mobilities' paradigm (Sheller and Urry 2006), which has turned attention to how mobile research methods can be used to understand everyday experiences through embodied, multi-sensory research experiences, walking interviews are becoming increasingly popular. They are particularly valued in giving some control to the participants who decide where to walk, and for creating enabling research environments (Ross et al. 2009). Jon Anderson (2004), for example, argues with others that identity both influences and is influenced by 'inhabited material places'. He suggests that conversations in place, or 'talking whilst walking', offer the potential to add new layers of understanding for the social scientist. He gives an example of his study of environmental activists, and the practice of taking a 'bimble', to walk or wander around aimlessly. Taking a participant off for a bimble gave both

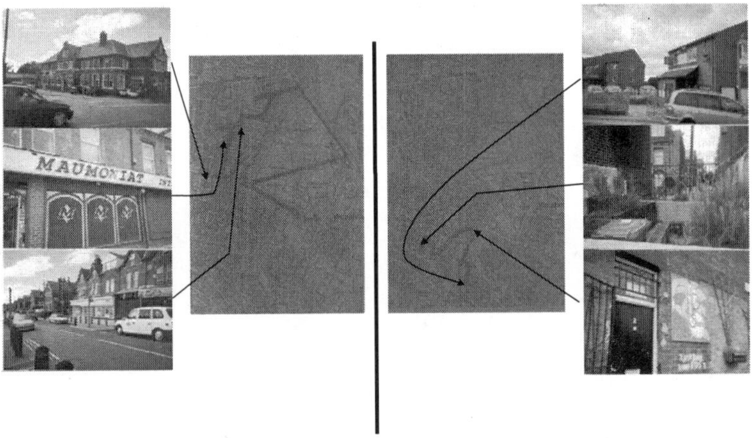

Figure 4.1 Routes and selected photographs taken on two walking interviews (Clark and Emmel 2010).

Reproduced with the kind permission of the authors.

a break from the tensions of the protest site, and offered a different point of access to his participants, evoking memories and connections from the place itself as well as his questions.

We have discussed the importance and potential effects on the research, participants and researcher of the setting in qualitative interviews. But there are interviews in which the researcher and participant are not in the same physical location.

Together and apart in time and space

In this section we discuss types of interviews where researcher and participant are separated in time and space. They might be in different time zones or separate locations at any distance apart. They could be responding to each other *asynchronically* via email or *synchronically* online via the appropriate software or instant messaging (Chen and Hinton 1999). They might use text as in these examples, or audio or video recorded responses. The researcher might be taking advantage of social networking sites (e.g. Facebook) to generate participants and conduct the interview (Snee 2008). Chat rooms and other virtual meeting places could be employed (Shepherd 2003). The researcher might undertake an ethnography of a virtual community (Beneito-Montagut 2011; Ethnography and Education 2013; Kozinets 2010). All of these possibilities change the nature, dynamic and space of the qualitative interview and raise further issues about research in virtual encounters (Hooley et al. 2012; Mann and Stewart 2000).

Telephone interviews: Landline and online

In telephone interviews the researcher and participant are each in, and in control of, their own separate space, and possibly at a considerable distance, although their exchange is *synchronous* in time. Different time zones might alter that experience of time and need specific arrangements. Advantages of the telephone interview are that it is cheaper, faster and, with participants who are hard to reach or located in difficult or dangerous places and spaces, safer. A wider geographical spread is possible. Neil Stephens (2007), located in the United Kingdom, used depth-interviews with elite macroeconomists located in the United States.

The telephone interview can be more acceptable to some participants when discussing sensitive topics, for confidentiality/privacy or convenience, for fitting into busy and complicated lives. Disadvantages include the lack of face-to-face contact and so lack of information about the other from their appearance, non-verbal communication in the interaction and the physical context. Amanda Holt (2010), using narrative interviews and critical realist discourse analysis, saw this lack of 'ethnographic' information on the participants' homes and selves as an advantage, enabling analysis at the level of the text. In her view, the lack of non-verbal communication similarly led to greater articulation from both researcher and participant in the exchanges.

Judith Sturges and Kathleen Hanrahan (2004) employed semi-structured interviews with visitors to county jail inmates and correctional officers who supervised the visit. Comparing the quality and amount of data generated and the quantity, nature and depth of the responses these researchers concluded that the findings did not differ substantially in the two methods. Those reluctant to take part face-to-face were pleased to be offered a telephone interview, valued being asked for their views and glad to give voice to issues about the system that bothered them. Although often researchers come to telephone interviews through problems in the research process, and had not previously considered the method, the comparative literature suggests that most found the telephone interviews productive and valid.

Technological development has led to the possibility of calls made online, with similar advantages to interviewing on a landline. Here a further possibility is visual contact (e.g. via Skype™ or Facetime™) where interviewer and interviewee can see each other, and perhaps part of their environment. Visual cues can become available once more, although not the full ethnographic possibilities. The interviewees must also have access to the necessary technology. Paul Hanna (2012) argues strongly that the benefit of using internet technologies such as Skype™ (low costs, ease of access, minimization of ecological dilemmas and the partial overcoming of issues of spatiality and physical interaction) make this a very valuable interview method. These and other rapidly developing modes of contact are expanding the scope and range of qualitative interviews (see too Chapter 8).

The e-interview

In an email interview there are similarly no constraints on location, the participants can be widely geographically separated, including worldwide. While an email exchange can be quite rapid, when using email for qualitative interviews, it is an advantage that the interviewer and interviewee are separated in time as well as space and the exchanges are likely to be *asynchronous*, with gaps of varying length between them. There are numerous advantages of the technique: it is written, producing text, obviating the need for transcription, saving time and resources, although this might lead to a less spontaneous account than produced in other interview methods. For the busy researcher and participant, the email interview offers considerable flexibility about when it takes place, with the participant in control of the flow, their response triggering the next communication from the researcher. The researcher can have several interviews running at the same time, and both researcher and participant can have time for reflection on the responses, and on the future direction of the research. Comparing the instantaneous response in online chat room exchanges, Jamie Lewis agrees that a written email response 'allows participants greater scope to think about any questions asked and, as such, often encourages more descriptive and well thought out replies' (Lewis 2006: 5). Time for consideration and reflection was also valued by Kaye Stacey and Jill Vincent using an electronic interview with multimedia hyperlinked stimulus resources with teachers of mathematics, seeking their beliefs, reflective observations and evaluations of mathematics teaching practice. This approach 'provided for a richer interview than would have been possible with a face-to-face interview in the more limited timeframe that would have been imposed' (2011: 605).

New skills are required of the e-interviewer not just technically being able to use email (a requirement for participants too) but for timing the flow of questions and judging how the interview is progressing when it is hard to assess the meaning of time gaps. Tactics need to be developed to deal with these issues, perhaps sending a slightly rephrased or amplified question (see Bampton and Cowton 2002 and application of their argument by Opdenakker 2006), or establishing ground rules at the beginning of the research about how long the exchanges will continue. In general it is better not to send all of the questions at once (although an indicative list of topics or issues sent early is useful) but to send them in the form of dialogue and exchange. The spatial separation might be advantageous, reducing the possibility of embarrassment for the participant and less obtrusive, and anonymity can be assured. This can raise ethical and other issues. Nalita James and Hugh Busher (2006) discuss problems of credibility, authenticity and other dilemmas in online interviewing.

As with all types of qualitative interview the email interview must produce data appropriate for your research questions, and both researcher and participant must have time and the appropriate software or equipment to pursue this option. Participants need to be comfortable writing about their experiences. Lucy Gibson (2010) undertook a qualitative mixed-method study of older music fans in three different music scenes (involving participant observation at music events and on virtual music discussion forums, as well as face-to-face or email interviews). Her email interviews took place over months, with long gaps between questions and responses, which varied widely in quantity of content. The process allowed participants to construct complex stories about their lives and experiences with music, having more in common with diaries than face-to-face interview data for Gibson, and the participants enjoyed 'authoring' their experiences.

Nicole Ison (2009) found email interviews useful for facilitating participation in research with people with impaired verbal communication. Her study used a narrative method to understand the experiences of young people with cerebral palsy, seeking their stories of emerging adulthood. Some of the young people who had verbal communication impairment wanted to take part in the research, and suggested that they could use email. Prior to the interview, Ison met participants, providing some familiarity with the participant and their environment. For Ison, 'the overwhelming value of this method is its capacity to facilitate participation by individuals who are unable to undertake face-to-face interviews' (2009: 170).

Self-interviews

In the self-interview the researcher is physically absent from the interview site, and the interviewee undertakes the interview in their own way in their own space. Emma Keightley and colleagues developed the 'self-interview' to use in the empirical study of memory, drawing on oral history approaches (Keightly et al. 2012). When piloting their study of practices of remembering, particularly about the 'life cycle' and stages in it, their participants associated photography and recorded music with memory and remembering. Initially using face-to-face interviews, the researchers realized that the participants needed more time to think, and to reflect on the memories elicited. They asked potential informants to record themselves talking about photos and recorded music and how these operated as vehicles of memory in their lives. The participants were provided with a guide sheet including the areas to be covered. Removing the interviewer enabled the participants to pause, think and reflect on their chosen images, and possibly to come to terms with any emotions evoked, choosing when to talk and for how long at any time. For these researchers self-interviews can capture the cross-temporal relation between the present in which the participants are remembering and the remembered past, exploring how the past is made sense of in the present.

Audio diaries have long been used in qualitative research. The participant can record their thoughts about their experiences as they occur, without the mediating presence of the researcher, similar to written diaries, but in a more immediate way that is possibly easier for the participant. Clearly, the topic of research and research questions will decide the appropriateness of this method. The researcher is of course guiding the research, is present in the imagination of the participant and can be addressed in the recording.

Lynn Monrouxe used solicited audio diaries in a longitudinal, narrative study of medical students to explore how they narrate their developing professional identity, moving from a 'human' gaze on the world at the start of training, to a predominantly 'medical' gaze at the end. She comments on the data: 'it was hard not to be impressed with the richness and diversity of the recordings, the ways in which the everyday and the extraordinary events experienced by these medical students became plotted into evocative constructions of their own developing professional narratives' (2009: 86). Monrouxe discusses her response to the emotional demands of some of the narratives she encountered, linked particularly to the longitudinality of the research, and draws attention to the similarity of the settings of the participant in producing and the researcher in reading transcribed diaries – although separate in time and space, both in solitude in the quiet of a room.

Conclusion

In this chapter we have considered the importance of the setting in which qualitative interviews take place and the effects this can have on interviewer and interviewee and their interaction, influencing the type of data that can be generated. These effects can be the most general – the influence of places and spaces on identity, perceptions, memories, emotions, the interaction of hierarchies of power at different levels associated with individuals, institutions, organizations, society. And they can be the very specific on the participants in the face-to-face interaction, including noise, interruptions, distractions. We have indicated the ideal space for the pragmatic qualitative interviewer, and discussed types of interviews where the research activity takes place at a distance through various technologies. In Chapter 5 we discuss the tools that can be used in qualitative interviews.

5 What sort of research tools can be used in conducting qualitative interviews?

Introduction

As we have stressed in this book so far, a key purpose of a qualitative interview broadly is to elicit the experiences, perceptions and feelings of the research participant/s – a sort of conversation or dialogue. It is an asymmetrical rather than an equal exchange, however. The interviewer largely delineates and controls the topic of discussion in an effort to, depending on your epistemological approach, gain access to essential meaning from, or co-generate it with, the interviewee or interviewees. Questions are the most commonly used interview tool in this endeavour, but researchers can utilize a range of other textual, visual and creative tools to engage interviewees and stimulate discussion as part of qualitative interviews, and thereby reveal aspects of participants' sense-making processes. Some argue that interviewees respond in a different way to these sorts of tools – that they access parts of personhood that interviews using words alone cannot reach.

Indeed, in addition to the relatively straightforward process of asking questions, there has been a proliferation of tools that researchers have developed to stimulate and facilitate interaction, enhance or contribute to communication and draw out (as desired) stories, accounts or responses. An interviewer can use many different techniques and tools as appropriate to the particular topic and questions of their research, the setting in which they are carrying out the interview as well as the form of the interview, and the characteristics of interviewees taking part in their research. In this chapter we begin by addressing the basic currency of qualitative interviews – talking – before moving on to address the sorts of techniques that researchers can use to augment and extend the process of asking questions: writing, seeing and creating. Under each of these broad headings we provide illustrations of work using these tools, albeit we can only discuss a few of the available techniques to illustrate their potential.

Talking

A basic tool for researchers in asking questions in qualitative interviews is an interview or topic guide. This guide is a list of questions or subjects that need to be covered during the interview, sometimes in a particular order and way (semi-structured), sometimes not (in-depth). The interviewer follows the guide, but as part of the exchange of talk during the interview is able to pursue topical trajectories that may stray from the guide when she or he feels this is fruitful and appropriate. Whether conducting a semi-structured or unstructured qualitative interview, in developing their question or topic guides researchers take into consideration: the focus of inquiry; what they want to learn from the person they are speaking with; how much time they have available and the kind of access they have; and how much they already know about their research topic.

The process of producing interview topics and questions for the guide, however, can seem mysterious. How does it occur? Where do you start? Kirstin Luker (2008: 168–171) provides an engaging and detailed description of how she generates interview questions and a guide:

> [I] take a pack of 3 by 5 index cards and write down every single question I want to know the answer to . . . I write one question per card, and I try to use the kind of easygoing, accessible language that I would use during an actual interview . . . So instead of writing 'What motivated you to get involved in this issue?' which is the real question I'm interested in, I would get at this with a number of questions, on the assumption that few of us know our own motivations, and even when we do, we rarely think of them as 'motivations' per se. So I would jot down a series of specific, concrete questions to get to this point: 'When did you decide to get involved? What was going on in your life? Why then, and not earlier or later? Why this issue and not a closely related one? . . .
>
> Then I take this stack of index cards . . . and I arrange them . . . I sit down near a flat surface – for me, the living room floor has always worked just fine – and I lay out these cards in different orders. If you play around with your cards long enough, you will see that they start to 'clump'. By this I mean that there will be a sort of topic outline of the areas you're interested in, and a series of questions

> will fall into each topic area. Then, within each topic area, I try to arrange the questions as closely as possible to an approximation of natural language . . . how would a natural conversation about your topic go? Obviously it would move from the more general to the more specific, and from the less emotionally threatening to the more emotionally threatening . . . [and at the end] you would want to 'cool down' the interview, setting the stage for a friendly departure.

Interview guides can be quite specific, covering types of questions and how they should be asked. A number of qualitative research texts provides typologies or categories of questions and their ordering, all of which can be useful in thinking about how to ask questions. James P. Spradley, in his classic text *The Ethnographic Interview* (1979), for example, identifies and describes a number of types of questions. These include descriptive-type questions such as broad, open 'grand tours' in the tone of 'tell me about your experience of . . .', 'what was it like being . . .', or questions where the interviewee is asked to talk through a specific concrete example of a situation, and so on. Another type of question is those that fall in the structural mode, for example, 'verification' sorts of questions about when, where and in what order something happened, or 'what do you mean by . . .' as well clarifications, etc. And contrast-type questions include the interviewer asking the interviewee to compare their experience of one issue or person with another, such as 'what's the difference between . . .', or rank or rate a range of experiences. We discuss more targeted types of interview questions and talking techniques, such as follow-ups and probes, further in Chapter 6 when we look at the practicalities involved in qualitative interviews.

In contrast to a detailed sequence of carefully thought-through questions, topic guides can be quite sketchy; more by way of a reminder of subjects to cover in the interview. The interviewer relies on the flow of interaction with the interviewee to steer the interview process, constructing questions about the issues to be covered as the interview progresses, rather than asking any predetermined specific types of questions. In Figure 5.1 we have reproduced a guide from a project that set out to understand the ways in which lone mothers might envisage the relationship between motherhood and paid work, which one of us carried out with a colleague, to show you what a topic guide of this sort might look like.

EXTRACT FROM: INTERVIEW GUIDE FOR LONE MOTHERS: PATTERNS AND PROCESSES IN UPTAKE OF PAID WORK

Household/Family Details:

Household composition – sex, age, ethnicity, relationship
Significant others – daily/intermittent
Education level
Route to/length of lone motherhood
Housing type and tenure

Paid Work:

Knowledge of local (area/neighbourhood) job availability
- how knows about them

Employment now and in past (why/why not)
- type/mode/length

Preference (why/why not)
Role of networks (opinion/decisionmaking)

Childcare:

Knowledge of local (area/neighbourhood) childcare availability (all types) – how knows about them
Use now and in past (why: use(d)/no longer/not using)
- type(s) (public/private/informal/father)
- mode(s) (days/hours/regularity)
- length(s) of use

Preference (why/why not)
Role of networks (opinion/decisionmaking)
If local informal childcare – similar/different (attitude/resources/household)

Networks: (network mapping)

Help – who/location/what/usefulness
Social life – group/individual
– adult/child orientation
– regularity/location

Figure 5.1 Topic guide used for Duncan and Edwards (1999).

Identity/Life Perceptions:

Self – as lone mother (same/different)
 – as paid worker
Problems/strengths of – lone motherhood
 – combining with paid work (if do)
How lone mothers viewed – society as a whole
 – locally

The key issue in thinking about talking techniques in interviews, though, is to come back to the fundamental issue of what the research is about. Certain types of questions will be better suited to promote interview interaction and discussion that provides answers relevant to the overarching subject of investigation, stimulating knowledge about the particular research issues as well as in keeping with the epistemological approach adopted (see Chapter 2). For example, descriptive 'grand tour' questions are an excellent fit with narrative research that seeks to elicit stories from interviewees and understand these within a broadly interpretive approach. The same issue of 'fit for purpose and approach' is true of the various types of research techniques and tools to augment and enhance interviews that we now discuss.

Writing

Written texts to stimulate talk in qualitative interviews can be produced either by the researcher or the interviewee before the interview for use during it.

A good example of researcher-generated writing to extend and enhance talk during an interview is vignettes. These are short stories or comic strips with a purpose; about characters in particular hypothetical but realistic circumstances or dilemmas that are relevant to the research enquiry. Interviewers ask interviewees to read them or read them to interviewees at a particular point in the interview and then ask them to comment on the situation. They are especially useful in research concerned with people's attitudes, beliefs and values. For example, along with colleagues one of us used vignettes in interviews with parents and step-parents, in a study of their understandings and experiences of parenting within and across households. We reproduce a vignette from this research as an illustration

> Ann has lived with Tony for the past two years, with her two daughters aged nine and seven from a previous relationship. Tony has recently been made redundant and, although Ann has a part-time job, money is tight. The children's father, Mark, has regular contact with them, and often takes them out and buys them expensive toys and clothes. Tony feels that Mark is splashing money around to show him up as not such a good father, while Ann feels that the girls are getting spoilt and are becoming too demanding at home. Ann briefly mentioned to Mark that he was spending too much on them, but he says they are his daughters and he should be able to provide them with the extra treats he'd buy them if they lived with him anyway.
>
> - What should they do? Why?
> - Have you ever been in a situation like this one? What happened?

Figure 5.2 Example of a vignette used in Ribbens McCarthy, Edwards and Gillies (2003).

in Figure 5.2. This particular vignette set out to explore the people's understandings of the relationship between material resources, household boundaries and parenting.

Vignettes are said to be especially useful in aiding interview discussion where topics are sensitive and interviewees may feel awkward talking about particular issues. Responding to vignettes can be an acceptable way of talking about private matters in the 'public' setting of an interview (Finch 1987).

Figure 5.2 is a relatively short and simple vignette. Janet Finch, however, developed the potential of the vignette technique further. She created a series of linked stories that she calls a 'soap opera style' of vignette that can be used in in-depth interview research as well as surveys. Discussion of the characters, dilemmas faced and options available to them in one vignette leads into another vignette in which the characters have moved on in their situation and thus face further dilemmas and options. Finch warns that three or four complex vignettes is the limit, otherwise the thread of stories and details can be difficult for interviewees to follow.

Written texts generated by an interviewee can be unsolicited or solicited. They can stand alone as research data but here we are concerned with their use as an aid in interviews. Where materials are unsolicited, they already exist prior to the research, say in the form of daily blog that can be followed up and discussed in an interview with the blogger. Solicited writing is produced specifically for the research. Researchers ask participants if they would undertake to produce the documents prior to the interview and give them instructions about how to do this. The texts are then used as the basis for discussion during a later face-to-face interview. Here we focus on solicited diary material as illustration of the potential of this technique.

Charlotte Kenten used solicited diaries coupled with diary interviews as a means of exploring the everyday positive and negative ways in which lesbians and gay men are made aware of their sexuality (2010). She asked her research participants to record daily, over a two-week period, whenever they became aware of their sexuality. She used this written method because she felt that such taken-for-granted experiences would be hard to capture in interviews alone. The A4 paper diary included a brief summary of the research on its first inside page, guidelines about completing the diary for the diary-keepers and the researcher's contact details. At the top of each of the 14 pages (one per day) there was a space for the date and several orientating prompt questions (see appendices in Kenten 2010). In the interviews subsequent to the two-week diary-keeping, the participants in Kenten's research reflected on the process of keeping a diary as well as explaining not only the contents that they might otherwise have not registered overtly but also their deliberate silences: what went unwritten, unrecorded and why. Kenton strongly argues that while diaries can be used as a stand alone method, where the diary keeping period is followed by an interview, entries made at particular points in time can be explored with their author (the interviewee) who can then explain and reflect upon their content. In this way, researchers can gain greater depth of understanding and insight on their topic of enquiry.

Seeing

As well as text, researchers can use images in interviews to facilitate talk – often referred to as elicitation. In this section we look at two elicitation techniques in particular: photos and graphics. Some argue that such visual images evoke deeper elements of human consciousness than do words and provide interviewers with a different order of participant responses, drawing out tacit knowledge, and latent memories and emotions (Harper 2002), which makes it attractive for researchers taking a psychoanalytic philosophical approach (see Chapter 2). There are also arguments that these visual elicitation techniques privilege the authority of the interviewee rather than the interviewer, fitting with an emancipatory approach (Harper 2002).

Photo elicitation

Photo elicitation is often thought of as a novel research tool, but in fact has a history stretching back into the mid-twentieth century as a technique used in anthropological studies. The use of photographs, or indeed other visual images (such as paintings, graffiti, advertisements, film clips), as a stimulus during qualitative interviews can draw on materials that are in existence prior to the research process and are brought to the interview either by interviewer or interviewee, or they can be generated specifically as part of the research process by the interviewee solely or in collaboration with the researcher. The photos may be general, collective or specific to the interviewee, and may be institutional (class of '79), of an era (farmers making hay in the 1930s), or intimate (family birthday party) (Harper 2002).

For example, drawing on participatory ideas, Jane Jorgenson and Tracy Sullivan (2010) asked children to take photographs of themselves or family members at home, working or playing with technology. They then explored what these images meant to the children through discussion in interviews, drawing out tacit qualities of family–technology relationships from children's perspectives that they argue would not otherwise be apparent. In contrast, Karen Henwood and colleagues (2011) used researcher-selected photo images of fatherhood from different eras (Victorian through to contemporary) in their longitudinal psychosocial study of men's accounts of first-time fatherhood. They asked their interviewees to comment upon these photos in interviews in an effort to understand the way in which the men formulated and made sense of their aspirations for modern fatherhood within and against dominant socio-historical representations of fathers.

Graphic elicitation

Graphic elicitation techniques cover a wide range of interview tools produced as part of qualitative interviews, to capture and represent relationships, feelings and so on. Timelines, for example, consist of a drawn line, straight or winding, representing time passing, along which interviewees mark significant events and aspects of personal experience over the course of their life as a whole or specific parts of it. Francis Guenette and Anne Marshall (2009) describe the use of interviewee-generated timelines in a narrative-based research project on the sensitive topic of the effects of domestic abuse on women's work lives. The authors argue that timelines enhance the narrative interview process, enabling interviewees to express themselves non-verbally, as well as providing a tool for interviewer and interviewee to aid reflection during the interview.

Graphic tools can also attempt to represent affect, using actual or metaphorical maps. Maps of a geographical area or location can be used in qualitative interviews to capture and talk about the emotions associated with different places and spaces. For example, researchers have asked children and young people to mark the spaces of safety and danger on a map of their local neighbourhood (Reay and Lucey 2002), or family members to place different coloured emoticon stickers on a floor plan of their home to indicate the spaces of family dynamics (Gabb 2008), such as ☺ to indicate happiness and laugher in the kitchen, and ♥ to indicate loving feelings in the hallway.

Metaphorically, as part of her groundbreaking anthropological study of households as resource systems, Sandra Wallman (1984) developed two linked network maps to use with interviewees. Each map consisted of concentric rings around the household unit with different segments or slices of the pie for kin, non-kin and difficult relationships respectively. Both maps recorded closeness of different kinds: one allowed the interviewee to record significant others in terms of geographical distance; the other recorded the same people in terms of their emotional closeness in the interviewee's view. Along with colleagues, one of us adapted a version of the emotional closeness and distance circle map to look at children and young people's understandings of biological and social ties (Edwards et al. 2006), using the template in Figure 5.3. The nearer to themselves at the centre of the circle that the interviewee places a named person, the closer emotionally they feel them to be. The interviewer can then discuss with interviewees why particular people are in particular positions on the map.

Most of these tools have been used with individual interviewees, but a graphic elicitation technique designed explicitly to capture interaction between research participants is Andrea Doucet's household portrait (2001). Doucet used this innovative tool to study gendered divisions of labour among heterosexual couples, enabling her interviewees to reflect on taken-for-granted routine and normally invisible patterns of behaviour.

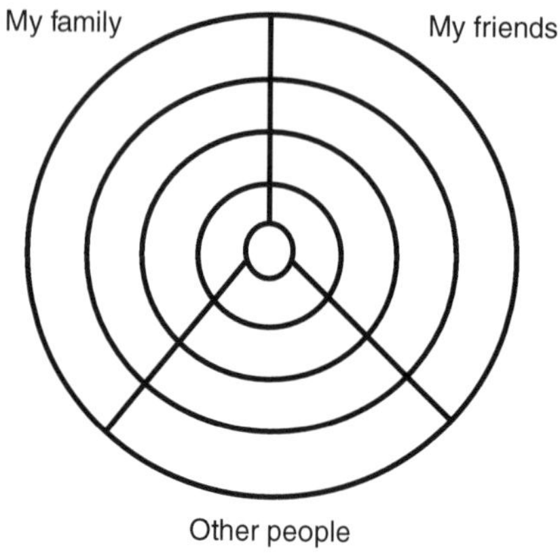

Figure 5.3 Template for an emotional closeness circle map used in Edwards et al. (2006).

The couple were asked to work together to place stickers with colour-coded household tasks and responsibilities onto a grid indicating whether and to what extent the activity was undertaken by the man or woman. The interviewer is present during this activity and can ask for, or be subject to, clarification or explanation as it happens. The graphic 'portrait' that results from the collaborative sorting of household tasks and responsibilities forms data in itself, but the couple's discussion together and with the researcher during the co-production is further, richer data.

Creating

All the interview tools discussed so far – talking, writing and seeing – are creative, but some tools can involve research participants in more extended and extensive projects that can be talked about in qualitative interviews in order to explore perceptions, emotions, memories, identities and so on. Here we provide three interesting examples to show the potential of creating techniques.

In a collaborative research team project, one of us has developed memory books as a method to be used alongside interviews in a qualitative longitudinal study of young people's transitions to adulthood (Thomson and Holland 2005). Such books go beyond the writing-a-diary tool described earlier. The research team provided their interviewees with a package containing a small book that could be used as a scrapbook as well as a diary, blank and trigger-word stickers ('love', 'myself', 'career', etc.), a folder for collecting paraphernalia, glue, a disposable camera, a leaflet explaining the purpose of the memory books and commenting on issues of ownership and confidentiality and so on. The memory books can stand alone as data, but they also served as a resource to facilitate another interview based on the material in the books stimulating discussion of the cultural resources and technologies that underpin young people's constructions of their selves.

Reality boxes for use in research with children is a tool conceived by Karen Winter as part of her research on children subject to local authority care orders (2012). She helped the young interviewees to decorate a shoe box using sparkling decorations, wool, pipe cleaners, lollipop sticks, pens, labels, pom poms and so on. The decoration on the outside of the box was a reflection of how they thought they came across to the outside world, while the inside contained constructions of their feelings and perspectives about their lives at home and in care. The boxes thus are metaphors for and by the child concerned.

The idea of 'metaphorical models', where interviewees are asked to make visual objects (video, collage, drawing, moulding, etc.) and then interpret them in interviews, has been propounded by David Gauntlett (2007), who has pioneered the use of lock-together plastic building bricks (part of LEGO™'s 'Serious Play' initiative) in this respect. People may, for example, be asked to create a model of how they feel on a Friday afternoon, or to build a model that overviews the different aspects of their identity. The research data are not only the creative product but also the discussion of the production process and choices made, and crucially the interviewees' interpretation of what they have produced. Gauntlett argues that metaphorical model creation is both embodied, in bringing mind and body together in order to explore experience, and empowering, in enabling people's creativity and trusting their ability to theorize themselves.

Conclusion

The research techniques for use in and with qualitative interviews that we have discussed in this chapter are not exhaustive. What we have done though, we hope, is to open the qualitative interviewer's mind to, and whet their appetite for, the possibilities and potential of a range of writing, seeing and creating tools to aid, stimulate, facilitate, enhance, draw out, augment, extend and contribute to talking. As well as not being exhaustive, the tools to use alongside talking are not exclusive. We have discussed writing, seeing and creating under separate headings, illustrated by their distinct use in particular studies, but they can be used in various combinations in a single project, depending on the research aims and the data needed to meet them. Whatever the techniques and tools used in qualitative interviews, however, careful questioning, listening and responding remains important – part of our concern in the next chapter.

6 What are the practicalities involved in conducting qualitative interviews?

Introduction

In this chapter we look at some of the practical issues involved in preparation for and during qualitative interviews. In other words, we address the practicalities of qualitative interviewing practice – the routine and taken-for-granted processes and activities that are part of the generation of interviews; what interviewers 'do'.

We cover preparation for interviews in terms of how many interviews need to be conducted, gaining informed consent for participation in interviews and equipment for recording interviews. And we deal with the mundane but crucial social interaction of conducting interviews: how to start an interview, how to listen and ask questions during an interview and how to finish an interview.

How many interviews?

Both students and more experienced researchers can be preoccupied with the question of how many interviews they should do when they are conducting a piece of qualitative empirical work. The topic frequently forms a thread on online discussion forums such as 'Methodspace' and 'Postgraduate Forum'.

The concept of saturation is often mooted as the ideal guide for the number of interviews to be conducted, especially where researchers are taking an interpretive, grounded approach. That is, qualitative interviewers should continue sampling and identifying cases until their interviewees are not telling them anything that they have not heard before. Thus rather than the number in a sample being representative of types of people as in quantitative research, in qualitative research it is the range of meanings that should determine numbers of interviewees in a study. Using data saturation is challenging for many qualitative interviewers, however, because sampling, data collection and data analysis have to be combined, and it is not possible to specify how many interviews are necessary in advance. This can be a problem where project proposals may require researchers to state a number.

A collection and review of advice from noted qualitative interview methodologists on the question of 'how many qualitative interviews is enough?' finds the recurring answer 'it depends' (Baker and Edwards 2012). The guidance offered by contributors as to what the number of interviews depends upon includes the following:

- *Epistemological and methodological questions* about the nature and purpose of the research: whether the focus of the objectives and of analysis is on commonality or difference or uniqueness or complexity or comparison or instances. A single case is sufficient if it is unique and not comparable, or to establish if something is possible, for example, but greater numbers are required to compare particular groups. A key issue is the ability to build a convincing narrative based on rich detail and complexity.
- *Practical issues* such as the level of degree, the time and finances available and institutional committee requirements. How much time is available to find and keep in contact with participants and complete the project, for example? And will research ethics committees or upgrade boards have a view on appropriate numbers?
- Linked to the last point, and cutting across epistemology and practicality, the judgement of the *epistemic community* in which a student or researcher wishes to be or is located is an issue. What size of sample or number of cases will satisfy mentors, peers and readers, and forestall critics? For example, one interview is considered valid evidence in oral history.

Some contributors to the collection do provide rough numbers to guide those who are desperate: 1 (Passerini; Sandino); between 12 and 60, with a mean of 30 (Adler and Adler); 20 for masters and 50 for doctoral theses (Ragin). Other examples of recommendations regarding how many interviews to conduct are Greg Guest and colleagues' (2006) argument that data theme saturation is achieved after 12 interviews, and Janice Morse's (1994) recommendation of a sample of 6 for phenomenological studies and 30–50 for grounded studies. This overall diversity in estimates of how many qualitative interviews are enough reveals the importance of the epistemological and methodological, practical and epistemic community issues that comprise the 'it depends' of the answer.

Information leaflets and consent forms

Most institutions require staff and students to gain ethical approval for their research before they begin their studies, and most social researchers regard fully informing potential participants about the research project in which they are being asked to participate, and gaining their informed – and often written – consent, as ethical good practice. For example, the research ethics committee of one of our institutions advises that information leaflets cover what the research is about, why the person has been chosen, what taking part in the study will involve, any benefits or risks involved, promises of confidentiality and anonymity, rights to withdraw, who to approach for further information or to complain to about the research process and so on. Similarly it is recommended that the consent form consists of a series of tick box statements about having read the information sheet, agreeing for their data to be used and stored for research purposes and their participation being voluntary, which the potential participant should then sign.

All social research is subject to debates about who can and should consent in the case of children or adults with learning disabilities; questions about whether consent can ever be *fully* informed where researchers themselves are not always sure what the outcomes and uses of the data may be before they start; discussion about whether consent is the one-off process implied by ethics committee processes; and concerns that the bureaucratization of consent procedures may shift research participation towards those who are comfortable with bureaucracy and signing forms (Edwards and Mauthner 2012; Miller and Boulton 2007; Wiles et al. 2005). Nonetheless, gaining informed consent in qualitative research also raises method-specific ethical issues in relation to interviewing.

In the case of interviews, potential interviewees usually are briefed about the purpose and process of the interview and how long it is estimated that it will last when invited to participate. Once they have agreed to participate, they are asked again for their consent at the start of the interview. Some, however, have concerns that being too specific about the topic and questions to be addressed in the interview may shape interviewees' answers in particular ways that may not be helpful to the research endeavour (Kvale

1996; see later for further discussion on this point). Certainly if you are interested in, for example, class prejudice among the elite it may not be a good idea to explain your research to them in those terms. Further, even if interviewees do have the research explained to them as fully as possible, consent can not be completely informed prior to an interview given that interviews may involve greater disclosure and revelation than both interviewee and interviewer anticipated or intended (Miller and Boulton 2007).

A more fundamental challenge is to be found in arguments that the qualitative interviewing process goes beyond explaining the substantive topic of the research and the type of questions to be asked in information leaflets because the interviewer him/herself is implicated in the process (unless an approach is adopted where the idea is to minimize the role of the interviewer as far as possible – see Chapter 2). Steiner Kvale points out the following in qualitative interviews:

> The person of the researcher is critical for the quality of the scientific knowledge and for the soundness of ethical decisions in any research project. By interviewing, the importance of the researcher as a person is magnified because the interviewer him-or herself is the main instrument for obtaining knowledge. (1996: 117)

Indeed, given Kvale's psychoanalytic philosophical approach (see Chapter 2), he is concerned with qualitative interviewers thinking through whether or not their interviews will touch on therapeutic issues (and if so what precautions can be taken), and issues of over-identification with interviewees.

Tina Miller and Mary Boulton take such ideas further, though, to argue that standardized regulation of consent procedures are increasingly ill-fitting for qualitative interviews conducted in a complex and fluid social world. Rather, they say, individual qualitative interviews need to be dealt with on their own terms, where the researchers should

> document the *process* of consent – the invitation, the response from the participant, the questions asked and answers given, the negotiation of dates and times of interviews, and so on. This is potentially a much more appropriate and useful way of working towards (and documenting) participation in research which is both informed and voluntary than asking participants to sign a consent form at the start of study. (2007: 2209, original emphasis)

In the case of qualitative longitudinal research, the fact that consent is a process is more apparent since it must be negotiated afresh for each research encounter.

Recording equipment

In qualitative interviews, words are the main currency of interviewing and subject to analytic interpretation; audio recording of interview talk has become standard. Audio recording interviewees may be impossible or inappropriate in some situations however, and sometimes interviewees may feel self-conscious about having their words recorded, or indeed the audio recorder may not work (or the interviewer cannot work it!). Interviews can still go ahead in these circumstances, with the interviewer making notes on what the interviewee says: recording talk in written note form.

Audio recording qualitative interviews can be useful both during the interview itself and afterwards. During the interview, recording the interview means that qualitative interviewers can focus on listening, probing and following up (see later) and maintaining eye contact with their interviewee. It can be quite distracting to have to keep making notes during the interview. But this is not to say that recording devices alleviate distractions from the talk of the interview. Interviewers can find themselves constantly checking whether or not their recording device is still working, if the microphones remain positioned closely enough to the interviewee/s to pick up their words clearly and monitoring the level of background noise (you may be able to focus on hearing the interviewee and mentally block out the music being played in the next room but the recorder will not).

As Ray Lee (2004) describes in his discussion of the history of the interview in relation to technological development and the implications for producing knowledge, as technologies develop, so do the means of recording qualitative interviews – from pen and paper notes and remembered quotes written up after the interview, to bulky reel-to-reel tape recorders, to portable cassette recorders, to mini digital audio recorders, and also video recorders. Sound quality has also improved. Since technology and the equipment available changes so rapidly, we do not cover specific devices here, but a useful list of factors to consider is provided in Figure 6.1.

- **Cost** (including batteries and media if applicable). Cheap recorders may mean increased transcription costs. Are batteries rechargeable?
- **Audio quality**. External microphones (mic-in jacks) are better than internal.
- **Ease of use**.
- **Portability** and **intrusiveness** in an interview situation.
- **Ruggedness** and **reliability** of recorder and media.
- Audio **recording format** and computer transfer.
- Length of **recording time** that media and batteries allow.
- **Information display** and control. Is the recording level displayed and can the recording level be manually adjusted? Is the remaining battery power and record time displayed?
- **Copy protection**. Is this implemented and what limitations does it impose?

Figure 6.1 Factors to consider in selecting digital audio recording equipment (Stockdale 2002).

Kirstin Luker explains that recording interviewees' words means that the metaphors or expressions and their emotional timbre and tone of voice during the interview – the way people say what they say – remains accessible long after the interview itself: 'Months and even years into a study, when I've finally figured out what the elements of my categories are, I go back to my very first interviews, and there they are, although my ear was not sophisticated enough to recognize them at the time' (2008: 174). And when it comes to writing up research, recording what an interviewee has said means that researchers can provide verbatim quotes.

This access to the talk of the interview through recording is not necessarily an unmitigated good. Some argue that the improvement of quality in interview recording devices can give a sense of being present at the interview later; a form of realist innocence (Ashmore and Reed 2002). Les Back muses on the recording of interviews as both enabling and limiting:

> Enabling in the sense that it allowed for the voices of people to be faithfully transcribed with accuracy. Paradoxically, the fact that the recorder captured the voice and the precise detail of what informants said meant that social researchers have become less attentive as observers. The tacit belief that the researcher needed merely to attend to what was said has limited the forms of empirical documentation. (2010: 23, 24)

Thus Back warns that qualitative interviewers need to think carefully about the analytic status they bestow on recorded accounts, and not fall into mistaking the socially shaped interview performance for a capture of the real and authentic (see also Atkinson and Silverman 1997, on the structure of the 'interview society' discussed in Chapters 1 and 2).

Starting an interview

You have your interviewee, consent has been gained, the recording device is working and the qualitative interview can start. But how is it best to begin? Luker recommends what she refers to as 'the hook' to start the conversation about the topic of research. The 'hook' is how she explains the study she is conducting to the people she is about to interview – yet again:

> Yes, I know that you probably used your hook when you talked to your interviewees on the phone to get them to agree to be interviewed; you may well have told them the hook when you first wrote them a letter asking if you could interview them; and there may even be a version of your hook in a consent form . . . But you can never tell people too often what your study is about, why you are interested in it, why *they* should be interested in it, and most important, why the person you are interviewing is *the* key person needed to help you understand this puzzling case that you are studying with such intensity. (2008: 171)

Once the stage for the interview has been set through the hook, qualitative interviewers often like to ask if the interviewee has any questions about the interview before they begin. They then open the interview 'proper' by asking general, broad questions of the 'grand tour' type mentioned in Chapter 5, for example: 'Please tell me how you started skydiving.' As the interview progresses, the questions gradually focus on more specific and targeted enquiries.

Listening, probing and following up

A qualitative interview is often thought about in terms of the interviewer asking questions and the interviewee responding to them. In this respect, Luker has the idea of 'turn signals' between different aspects of the research topic that comprise the interview, which alert the interviewee that you are shifting from the issue that you have just asked them about and they are currently discussing, to another area of the research topic. An example that she gives is: 'Up to now, we've been talking about your childhood. Now I'd like to ask you about [fill in the blank]' (2008: 170–171). But interviewees are not just passive respondents, and interviewers have to fit themselves around what the interviewee is telling them and respond in turn with appropriate questions that fit into the 'natural' flow of the discussion.

Indeed, overall the process of qualitative interviews requires a lot of concentration and effort on the part of the interviewer. As Jennifer Mason (2002: 45) explains:

> At any one time you may be: listening to what the interviewee(s) is or are currently saying and trying to interpret what they mean; trying to work out whether what they are saying has any bearing on 'what you really want to know'; trying to think in new and creative ways about 'what you really want to know'; trying to pick up on any changes in our interviewees' demeanour and interpret these . . .; reflecting on something they said 20 minutes ago; formulating an appropriate response to what they are currently saying; formulating the next question which might involve shifting the interview onto new terrain; keeping an eye on your watch and making decisions about depth and breadth given your time limit.

Listening and attending to what interviewees are saying is a crucial skill for a qualitative interviewer as part of the social interaction of interviews. It involves being attuned, alert and attentive to what the interviewee is telling you, or even not telling you. Listening well is a qualitative interviewing skill that often goes unremarked in favour of a focus on how to ask questions, yet it is the foundation of being able to respond to what the interviewee is saying, and able to probe and follow up their answers to your questions effectively and sensitively.

Probing and following up in interviews are means by which qualitative interviewers attempt to get an interviewee to open up, provide more information, elaborate and expand on what they have said. It is difficult to plan probes in advance because they are responses to what an interviewee is saying at the time in the interview, but it is useful to have a sense of the range of probes that a qualitative interviewer can use. H. Russell Bernard

(2000) delineates seven ways of probing during qualitative interviews, most of which require prudent and well-judged use at different points within a single interview:

- *Silence.* This probe involves being quiet once an interviewee appears to have finished answering a question, perhaps nodding your head, and waiting for an interviewee to continue and add more to the topic they were discussing. It provides interviewees with time to reflect. Allowing silence to endure in an interview can be very difficult for interviewers, but effective if used sparingly.
- *Echo.* This is where an interviewer repeats the last point that the interviewee has said, and is useful especially when they have been describing a process or event. Bernard asserts that this probe shows the interviewee that you have understood what they have said so far and encourages them to continue and expand.
- *Uh-huh.* Saying 'yes', 'I see', 'right' and so on as an interviewee talks affirms what the interviewee has said. It can act rather like silent nodding of your head.
- *Tell-me-more.* After an interviewee has answered a question, this probe encourages interviewees to expand and go further through follow on questions along the lines of 'Why do you feel like that about it?' 'Can you tell me more about that?' 'What did you mean when you said . . .?' 'What did you do then?' etc.
- *Long question.* These sorts of probes can help at the beginning of interviews in the grand tour mould. Bernard gives the example of when he asked sponge divers he was interviewing, 'Tell me about diving into really deep water. What do you do to get ready, and how do you ascend and descend? What's it like down there?' (2000: 198). He also says that threatening or sensitive questions (he gives the example of condom use) can benefit from a long rambling run up to them.
- *Leading.* These are directive probes – though as Bernard points out, any question leads in an interview. The idea of asking leading questions is often treated in introductory methods textbooks for students as if it were an anathema, with concerns about 'bias'. The assumption is that if you ask a leading question then the answer you get will be produced by the way the question is put: such as 'do you think that this is a really bad way of behaving?' Qualitative interviewers with experience, however, know that this is rarely the case. Interviewees

are perfectly capable of telling you that you do not understand what they mean; that actually they don't 'think it's a really bad way of behaving' at all.

- *Baiting.* Bernard says this sort of probe is a 'phased assertion' in which the interviewer acts as if they already know something. He contends that either people then feel comfortable opening up or are likely to correct you if they think that you have got the wrong idea.

Bernard also provides advice on dealing with interviewees who either say too much or too little during an interview. 'Verbal' interviewees are very likely to go off at a tangent as they tell you much more than you need to know for your research topic. He recommends 'graceful' interruption and moving the interview back on track. 'Non-verbal' interviewees provide monosyllabic or 'don't know' responses to questions. As Bernard says: '[S]ometimes you can get beyond this, sometimes you can't.' If you can't, then it is best to 'cut your losses' (2000: 200). Indeed, often qualitative interviewers can feel themselves to be failures if they have to give up on an interview but this is not the case. There is little to be gained by continuing on for the sake of it and ending an interview may sometimes be the wisest course of action.

Finishing an interview

By the time an interview ends, qualitative interviewers will probably have spent an hour or more asking their interviewee/s questions and the interviewees will have been telling them about their lives. This can create a sort of intimate link that is broken suddenly when the interview ends. Luker (2008) discusses the 'cool down' to 'finish up and let go of the interview' that enable both interviewer and interviewee to detach themselves from each other gradually, through final questions that focus on the future or ask the interviewee to review their experience or identify the most important thing that they feel they have discussed or mentioned. It is also important finally to thank the interviewee. Luker warns, however, that it might be an idea to keep your audio recorder handy at this point because sometimes interviewees can start opening up again with fascinating information just after the recorder has been turned off. Such a practice, however, has ethical dimensions (Wiles 2012) – does the participant need to consent explicitly to the further recording of their words after they may assume that the research interview has finished.

The discussion of practicalities in this chapter may seem rather mechanistic at points (e.g. probes such as repeat the point the interviewee makes). Interviews can be situations of visceral dynamics, however, involving power and emotions – as we discuss in the next chapter.

7 What are the power and emotional dynamics of qualitative interviews?

Introduction

Issues of power and emotion in social research generally, and within the qualitative interview situation especially, have been the subject of attention in the methods literature for some time, across a range of philosophical approaches. In qualitative interviewing, researchers attempt to create an interaction that goes beyond a conversational exchange, where their interviewees feel safe enough to talk openly about their experiences and understandings. To some extent then, researchers attempt to exercise power to generate an atmosphere in which interviewees will experience emotions of rapport that are beneficial for the interview. But researchers also pay attention to the dynamics of power and emotions in interviews because they are concerned about the ethics of the research process, as well as the insights into the topic under investigation that such reflection can generate. These two sides of interviews have been termed 'conquest or communion', with interviewers exercising power though the application of questioning techniques such as probing in order to generate data from interviewees (see Chapter 6), but also experiencing an emotional interdependency with their interviewees (Ezzy 2010).

From a psychosocial perspective in particular, power and emotions come together in both conscious and unconscious ways in a qualitative research interview. As noted in Chapter 2, at the heart of a psychoanalytic perspective on the interview is the notion of a 'defended subject'. In this view, anxiety is inherent in the human condition and consequently unconscious defences against anxieties come into play for both interviewee and interviewer and are part of the dynamics of the interview (as in all types of relations between people) (Hollway and Jefferson 2012). But power and emotions are also present in everyday lives and interactions in a more social-structural, relational manner. Society consists of groups of people sharply divided from one another. Social divisions refer to social patterns of substantial and distinctive material and cultural differences between people – around race, social class sexuality, religion and so on – where the social positioning of members of certain categories is better than others, giving them a greater share of resources and power over the way that society is organized (Payne 2006). These hierarchies and inequalities can shape and be traced in interview interactions.

In this chapter we consider some of the dynamics of power asymmetries and interplays of emotion discernable when interviewer and interviewee come together in the qualitative interview situation.

The dynamics of power in interviews

By its nature interview research involves asymmetries of power; it is the interviewer who defines the situation and who frames the topic and course of the interview (Kvale 1996). But the situation is more complex than this. The minimal structure of an in-depth qualitative interview in particular invites and enables multifaceted power shifts between interviewer and interviewee across the course of an interview. Elizabeth Hoffman describes this as 'the interview dance', and details some of the basic steps:

> The researcher will initiate contact, a somewhat powerful gesture, but then the interviewee might have strong preferences as to where and when to meet . . . Once the interview actually takes place, the interviewer begins by asking questions . . . The researcher's questions, however, are of little value without the responses from the interviewee. Here, again, the power shifts back to the respondent. Interviewees might condition their replies on various responses of the interviewer . . . Sometimes the interview process itself can seem threatening [to the interviewee]. (2007: 337)

Integral to the interview dance is the power of knowledge: who is a knowing and approving expert and who is a vulnerable knowledge seeker. Hoffman describes some exchanges in her research with homecare workers looking after elderly or sick clients in which these positions shifted around:

> Occasionally the homecare workers I interviewed felt 'exposed' and wanted my reassurance that the responses and actions they described to me were appropriate and professional. This put me in the role of confessor and, perhaps, therapist, as they told me how

> they dealt with situations that were emotionally difficult for them. While, on the one hand, this vulnerability might have made the interviewee feel less powerful and threatened by my questions . . ., it also thrust them into a more powerful role: I needed to successfully fulfill the role of therapist and confidant before the respondent would move the interview forward. (2007: 338)

Hoffman's describes such interview encounters as involving the interviewer in extensive emotional labour (a topic we return to later) which in itself demonstrates the power of the interviewee in the interview relationship.

So far we have been concerned with the way that power can shift around over the course of an interview as a result of the positioning of both interviewer and interviewee within the interview situation itself. However, we also need to take into account the way that social divisions and hierarchies around class, gender, race/ethnicity, age and other aspects of social status articulate with this situation and further mediate power relations (see too Chapter 4). Here we consider marginality and elite group membership. A recurring theme is the extent to which interviewers are insider members or outsider non-members of the interviewee group.

Interviewing members of marginalized groups

Quite a lot of interview research is carried out with social groups who are marginalized in society. Indeed some time ago Colin Bell characterized empirical sociology as 'done *on* the relatively powerless *for* the relatively powerful' (1978: 25; original emphases). Some argue that a focus on the interview accounts of marginalized groups serves only to perpetuate their exclusion and increase perceptions of them as problematic, confirming and legitimizing the status quo of inequality (Biggs 2003). But researchers can feel a commitment to making audible what they regard as the 'silenced' voices and perspectives of the marginalized, for example, those who are working from feminist or emancipatory approaches that seek to minimize the power differential in the research setting (see Chapter 2).

The implications of an interviewer's 'positionality' (social status and identity) in relation to an interviewee is a key focus of discussions, with recurring themes being how social divisions between interviewer and interviewee may shape an interview, and the extent to which unspoken assumptions are a feature of interviews where interviewer and interviewee share membership of a marginalized group. In this section we look first at situations where an interviewer may or may not share a marginalized status with their interviewee – gender and race/ethnicity – before moving on to situations where in the past they may have been positioned similar to their interviewees in terms of social class or age but no longer can be. This is by no means a comprehensive coverage of marginalized groups (e.g. see Melanie Nind 2008, on interviewing and other qualitative methods with people with disabilities), but it does highlight some general issues of power in interviews.

As we have noted already there is a considerable literature about power issues and gender in interviews. Several decades ago, in a highly influential article, Ann Oakley challenged the paradigm of the research interviewer as objective and detached, disengaged from the interviewee on a personal level. She argued that in a situation where interviewer and interviewee were women, they were both 'inside the culture' of being women in a male-dominated society and engaged with each other on that level: 'A feminist interviewing women is by definition both "inside" the culture and participating in that which she is observing' (1981: 53). Oakley also presented the feminist interview as a non-hierarchical exchange. Across the years, other feminists have raised concerns about the way that this very connection could be to the detriment of interviewees, where rapport is used instrumentally to draw them out in order to get 'good data' (Cotterill 1992; Duncombe and Jessop 2007; Finch 1984). We return later to the point about the danger of exploitation being inherent in pursuing rapport in the section discussing emotions in the interview process.

Yet other social divisions articulate with gender, such that women are not all similarly socially positioned nor sharing cultural experiences. In particular, race and ethnicity has been the subject of attention in the interview situation, with debates about whether or not interviewers who are researching people from minority ethnic backgrounds need to share 'race' with their interviewees in order to generate 'better' or more 'authentic' data (e.g. Bhavnani 1993; Bhopal 1997; Phoenix 1994). For example, one of us has discussed the way that race infused the research relationship where she, as a white woman, was interviewing black women and argued that acknowledging racial difference was important to establishing rapport (Edwards 1990).

Even where interviewee and interviewer share membership of a marginalized minority group, however, social divisions and power are not eradicated. For example, Tracey Reynolds (2004) has discussed how her stress on her 'sameness' with her second/third generation British-born Caribbean interviewees could nonetheless mean that she was quizzed extensively about her personal background as well as the nature and purpose of her research. She places this in the context where the Caribbean community in Britain has a sophisticated understanding of a research process that tends to problematize and create misconceptions about the Black community. Minelle Mahtani also challenges any simplistic notions of shared identities between interviewers and interviewees on the basis of race in a critical reflection on her own research process in a study of mixed-race women. While she and interviewees shared rapport and expectations of mutual recognition around mixedness, she shows how these are cross-cut with various social cleavages that separated them. Mahtani also reveals the potential drawbacks of similarity for the interview as a data generating process:

> During the research process, there were certainly times when my own status as a mixed-race woman of Indian and Iranian descent did foster dialogue . . . During a pivotal point in our interview, one participant explained to me how she felt comfortable talking to me as a woman of mixed race . . . However, at the same time, I was well aware that my own identification as a woman of mixed race played other roles in the interview process. For example, peppered through many interviews emerged the phrase, 'you know what I mean, Minelle' followed by a knowing glance or smile. This sort of shared complicity may have created a more comfortable space for these women to tell their stories – but also prevented them from divulging further detail. (2012: 158–159)

Many researchers from working-class backgrounds, including Val Gillies, have pointed out: 'My education and salary mean I can no longer claim to be working class' (2004: 17). Gillies discusses how as a consequence of moving into higher education and an academic career she has gradually been detached from the day-to-day context that frames the lives of her working-class family and friends, but that what she is left with is a commitment to making her marginalized interviewees' voices heard through the collection and presentation of interview data (see also Skeggs 1997: 14–15).

Similarly, while researchers may once have been children and young people, they no longer are. As with Gillies, though, those undertaking interview-based research with what they consider to be a marginalized social group – children – are often motivated by a desire to counter wider societal silencing of their voices, from an empowerment perspective (see Alderson and Morrow 2004; Greene and Hogan 2005; MacNaughton et al. 2010). For example, Pauline Davis (2007) argues that the storytelling technique that she used in interviews with children is a democratic, socially inclusive approach. She asked 7–8 year-old children who were 'poor readers' to recount a story about 'The child who didn't like reading'. Davis asserts that this technique shifts the equilibrium towards the storyteller, and leads the interviewer to take on a less dominant role, and illustrates this with two contrasting interview extracts from a boy called Dominic (175):

Pauline: And why do you think children read?
Dominic: Because they like reading.
Pauline: So what do you think it is that they like about reading then?
Dominic: They like the books!? [*questioning intonation*]
Pauline: Can you think of anything else?
Dominic: [*thinking*] I don't know. My Nana's got a new kitten; shall I tell you about it?

Compare Dominic's use of language in the extract above with a story I asked him to tell me, titled 'The child who didn't like reading':

> The boy who didn't like reading was reading his library books. Boys picked on him and then he didn't like it. A boy who didn't like reading was so behind and then he didn't like reading forever so he didn't take his reading book home so he didn't read. He was behind with the lower books. Mum said: 'Where is your reading book?' The boy said: 'I left it at school because I don't like reading any more.'

For Davis, the storytelling method during an interview raises the status of children though demonstrating how power can shift as they shape the interview themselves in a context where adult power over children is likely to complicate the interaction that takes place during an interview.

Interviewing members of elite groups

In contrast to the situation where a researcher has more power than the people they are interviewing, at least in the context of wider society, it is the other way around in what is sometimes referred to as 'studying up'. Just as researchers can feel a commitment to 'giving voice' to powerless groups, they can also regard it as important to demystify the worlds of people in positions of power and privilege in society.

Those with experience of interviewing elites often emphasize the need for interviewers to have 'done their homework' before the interview and be well-prepared for it, in terms of familiarizing themselves with interviewees' background and career, or the company that they represent, and/or their published views and so on, as well as ensuring that they have an in-depth grasp of the key issues concerning the topic under discussion (e.g. Mikecz 2012; Phillips 1998). Such strategies are regarded as a means for the researcher to attempt to decrease the status imbalance between themselves and their interviewee, and to position themselves as someone who can be considered equal in terms of situated knowledge.

Several writers mention that interviewers will find themselves subject to subtle probing about their agenda and intentions for use of the interview data, and Karen Ross (2001) even found that a few of the women MPs she interviewed in Australia and South Africa audio-recorded the interview themselves (in addition to Ross's own recording for research purposes). Interviews with elite groups are often posed as a power game in which both interviewer and interviewee jockey for the upper hand. The interviewee is seeking to set the agenda and create a 'discourse within which research becomes enmeshed and to a considerable degree reproduces' (Fitz and Halpin 1994: 40), while the interviewer attempts control through asking their questions.

Researchers can take different positions on how best to ensure that they are not intimidated or overwhelmed, and to follow their own research agenda rather than that of their participants. Karen Duke found a set of tools of the profession helpful in asserting authority in her interviews with policymakers in the criminal justice field: 'bringing along a typed topic guide which was always visible to the respondent, and being prepared with pen, paper, clipboard and tape-recorder. Armed with these props, I felt better able to retain control by ensuring that my agenda was covered during interviews' (2002: 53). Ross, though, regards finding common ground on which to build trust as important in oiling the wheels of talk and disclosure in interviews (see also Klatch 1988):

> I adopted slightly different modes of being and modes of saying which were mostly contingent (but not exclusively so) on my interviewee's

> political 'colours'. Thus with the socialist women, I nearly always introduced somewhere into the conversation the fact that I was politically active in my local Labour Party. This disclosure almost always elicited an immediate interest in what I had been doing and questions about my own political career and future. With the Liberal and Tory women, I did not use such a strategy but found alternative points of identification: often our shared gender and experiences as women in male-oriented professions was a salient and important feature of developing good rapport. (Ross 2001: 162)

In contrast to the power battles portrayed by some interviewers of elite groups, Ross asserts that her women MP participants usually were courteous and helpful, and puts this down to their shared gender. On the basis of her interviews with right-wing women active in the conservative movement in the United States, Rebecca Klatch (1988) believes that young female interviewers in particular may have an advantage in being perceived as non-threatening and eliciting open accounts, and also argues that a 'non-argumentative approach' on the part of the interviewer is important. However, Roslyn Mickelson (1994) fears that this type of rapport-building can result in bland, public relations type responses. She thus advocates asking blunt questions of powerful interviewees such as the education policymakers she interviewed, and challenging any evasive answers. Both age and gender play important parts in 'interviewing up', and being a young woman, for example, can also result in older male participants wanting to exercise control and exert power. This reaction, as noted later, is not limited to 'interviewing up'.

The status positioning of powerful people within society means that, on the one hand, they are familiar with being asked their opinion, talking and being listened to – though as we note above, not necessarily answering the questions that they are being asked. Yet, on the other hand, elite interviewees may also be subject to formal constraints on disclosure such as the Official Secrets Act, or informal rules of political, administrative or corporate reputation and loyalty and an 'official line' to be put forward. Both have implications for what they are prepared to say in qualitative interviews. John Fitz and David Halpin (1994) reflect on their interviews with civil servants involved in national education policymaking: they only ever accessed a partial and incomplete picture. This is likely to be the case to varying extents with any interview – the point is to be aware of it.

Several researchers who discuss conducting research interviews with members of social, economic or politically powerful groups mention variously being comfortable with or excited by their high status participants, feeling grateful to them or steam-rollered by them, feeling privileged or patronized, and/or impressed or uncomfortable about betraying their own beliefs and position. This raises the issue of emotions in the dynamics of interviews.

The dynamics of emotions in interviews

By virtue of being human, researchers are not neutral and objective enquirers in qualitative interviews but are emotionally engaged participants who are sharing an experience with the interviewee. Indeed, those taking feminist and interpretive approaches to scholarship have questioned the binary opposition between reason and emotion in much Western thought, and argued that emotion is necessary to knowledge – people make sense of the social world through emotions as well as cognition or intellect (e.g. Game 1997; Jaggar 1989). One of us (Holland 2007, 2009) has reviewed discussions of the different ways that emotions can and do come into the research process, and notes how important acknowledgement of and reflection on these emotional dynamics can be for the production of knowledge. Key themes from that review that relate to interviews that we pursue here are:

- the importance of emotions in interviews, both those of the interviewee and the interviewer;
- the considerable amount of emotion work called for in qualitative interviews, and the potential dangers consequent on this.

The open-ended qualitative interview, with its possibilities for discussing unexpected topics, means that emotional dynamics can be significant for the interview process. Hoffman notes one of her dilemmas: 'How would my displays of emotion affect my informants' abilities to share the emotional components of their stories? If I shared too much of my own emotions, would I silence them? If I shared too little emotion, would I appear unresponsive, hostile, or unable to understand their predicaments?' (2007: 340). Maxine Birch and Tina Miller point out that qualitative interviewers often work with an understanding of a 'good' interview as one in which they elicit a particular style of narration from their interviewee, involving self-disclosure: 'as interviewers we need to try to suspend the belief that a more personal story reveals a more authentic story' (2000: 200). As we noted earlier, several researchers express concern about the way that the interviewers' exercise of emotional research skills, used to 'invite intimacy' through creating rapport and an atmosphere of disclosure, runs the risk of exploiting research participants.

But researchers can also feel contaminated with the emotional effort of creating rapport, and the emotional management work required to elicit interview accounts. For example, Shaminder Takhar (2009) has described how her interviews with conservative Muslim South Asian women about 'covering up' in dress involved her 'covering up' her own emotional responses to the content of those interviews. Of one woman interviewee's assumptions about shared Asian-ness meaning shared values, Takhar writes:

> [She] was under the impression that I would understand what she meant. Far from identifying with these women on the basis of being South Asian, I had distanced myself from such a position. I left this interview agitated as I had not expected such statements to be made [that western women invite rape through their provocative dress] and neither had I responded to them . . . I felt my feminist principles were compromised and wondered why I had endured it. I had not responded to them . . . I had made a judgment on the need to acquire data . . . When I left the venue, I felt an enormous weight lifting off my shoulders because during the interview I had felt suffocated. (2009: 35)

In contrast, there are also dangers in empathy and engagement, and some voice concern about the emotional cost for researchers in undertaking interviewing people who may tell stories redolent with grief, loss, anger and resentment (Bloor et al. 2007; Dickson-Swift et al. 2006; Hubbard et al. 2001; Watts 2008). As well as sensitive topics that concern death, violence and so on, more mundane subjects can raise both conscious and unconscious emotions for interviewer and interviewee. Helen Lucey and colleagues (Lucey et al. 2003: 281) have described what they regard as unconscious negative transferences between Helen and a couple she interviewed, Mr and Mrs Green, as part of a qualitative longitudinal study of girls growing up:

> Helen's request for Mr and Mrs Green to engage with the idea of their daughter Erica one day leaving home provoked some unconscious anxiety in them indicated by the difficulty they had in imagining it.

Helen: Just talking about Erica's independence, can you see her moving away from home and living independently? Sooner or later?

Mrs Green: No.

Mr Green: I don't know. Maybe when she marries. I don't know, it depends.

Mrs Green: We've been told that we're not allowed to sell the house and when me Mum's gone Darren's going to have this side, because it's a bigger house and Erica's going to have that side, and we're going in an old peoples home. *(laughs)*

Helen: One up the road? *(laughs) (Mr and Mrs Green laugh)*

However, this discussion was not only making Mr and Mrs Green anxious. It is at this point that Helen's own unconscious anxieties got the better of her and forcibly made their presence known.

Mr Green: I can't see her moving away to work. Is that what you mean?

Helen: For any reason? I mean, one of my fantasies when I was 16 was to get away as soon as possible and live in a bedsit.

Although consciously feeling 'connected' with the Greens on more than one level, their resistance to the idea of Erica leaving home provoked in Helen intense feelings of being trapped.

Thus for qualitative researchers, the emotional dynamics of interviews can be intensely personal, as for Lucey and the resurrection of her feelings as a young woman living at home, but also socially informed processes, as with Takhar's judgement about covering up to hear data about covering up.

Again and again, researchers writing about the power and emotions in qualitative interview research argue that attending to their existence and dynamics can only enhance the knowledge generation process. Such reflection will enhance researchers' understanding of the data and their insights into the nuances of the research topic.

Conclusion

In this chapter we have considered some of the asymmetries of power and generation of emotions in interviews. We considered how the cross-cutting social positions of both interviewer and interviewee can shape and shift power dynamics during the interview in complex ways, and the gamut of emotions and emotion work that interviewing can generate and involve for both parties. Along the way, we have noted how reflecting on the dynamics of power and emotions in the interview process can provide insight about the substantive research topic. In the next chapter, we step back to the part that qualitative interviews play in the knowledge generation endeavour more broadly. We consider the strength of this method, the challenges it has and is facing and what the future might hold.

8 What are the strengths, challenges and future of qualitative interviews?

Introduction

Throughout this book we have emphasized that it is important for the researcher to have an awareness of the philosophical and epistemological position that underlies the qualitative interview and qualitative research in general. In Chapter 2 we briefly considered the history of the qualitative interview, and evaluated assertions that qualitative interviews and research have passed through eight or nine 'moments' since 1900 (Denzin and Lincoln 2011). We saw that there are overlapping and intersecting approaches in the moments of this model, there is no linear progression; we can say then that all of the underpinning philosophical positions upon which qualitative interviews are based that we then described in that chapter are currently in play. We did suggest a progression in the terms used to describe the person interviewed, which was seen to reflect the changing relationship between researcher and researched, interviewer and interviewee, and a growing reflexivity from the researcher, under the influence of some of the philosophies outlined, particularly feminist and postmodern approaches (Chapter 1).

This book is based on an understanding of the value and importance of qualitative interviews and their contribution to a social scientific understanding of social events and interactions in context in the social world. But there are challenges to this position. In this concluding chapter we will discuss the strengths of qualitative interviews and the challenges faced by the qualitative interview method; challenges facing the method in the current context, which might be threats to its continuing use; and what the future might hold, as well as summing up the key message of this book – 'what is qualitative interviewing?'

Strengths

Paul Atkinson and David Silverman (1997) argued that we are in an interview society where interviews have become a fundamental activity, and crucial to people's understanding of themselves (see Chapter 1). Giampietro Gobo sees ethnography as an increasingly popular qualitative method, and suggests:

> If the 'interview society' is still the dominant societal model, the recent sudden increase of ethnography can be explained with the hypothesis that we are entering a[n] 'observation society', a society in which observing (as interviewing) has become a fundamental activity, and watching and scrutinizing are becoming important cognitive modes alongside the others, like listening, feeling, hearing and eavesdropping, typical of the 'interview society'. (Gobo 2011: 48)

We could suggest that both exist and interact in the current moment, and it has been argued more generally that we are in a cycle of increased acceptance of qualitative interviews and other qualitative methods (Gobo 2005; Holland et al. 2006). Malcolm Williams and Paul Vogt offer reasons for the increasing popularity of social research methods in general: the end of the paradigm wars; the development of mixed methods approaches (or methodological pluralism); technological developments; statistical and scientific developments; and greater publishing opportunities (2011: 4). Other explanations for the increasing popularity of qualitative interviews offered are recognition of a need for methods that can give insight into the meanings that individuals and groups attach to experiences, social processes, practices and events, for example, by policy decision makers. This has led further to the realization of the value and relevance of qualitative research and findings from interviews for practice in various policy areas, including welfare, health and education, and in some instances for the value of qualitative longitudinal research to be recognized, placing policy changes in the context of people's lived experience (Holland et al. 2006; Molloy et al. 2002; Neale et al. 2012).

Jennifer Mason (2002: 1) lists some of the strengths of qualitative interviews that are sometimes lost from sight, arguing that through them we can explore:

- the texture and weave of everyday life;
- the understandings, experiences and imaginings of research participants;

- how social processes, institutions, discourses or relationships work; and
- the significance of the meanings that they generate.

We have seen from the discussion in this book that the qualitative interview method has been evolving, taking on board criticisms to strengthen research interviewing practice, incorporating technological change, using visual and other methods within the interview to enhance the process of knowledge production (see Chapter 5). The method can provide depth and detail to the more general picture/viewpoint offered by quantitative social data, and so qualitative interviews can form a crucial part of complex multi-modal studies, combining multiple qualitative methods, or multiple qualitative and quantitative methods; in the longitudinal context when following participants through time, they can provide a way into uncovering complex processes of causality.

Challenges

Any piece of qualitative research and any qualitative interview can be criticized from a number of perspectives, and just as with any type of research method, not all qualitative interviews constitute good research. What we have pursued in this book is good practice in understanding and undertaking qualitative interviews within the framework of a well-specified philosophical and epistemological position. Qualitative interviews undertaken in this way would escape the more ill-informed criticisms of qualitative research that have been made, for example, that it is anecdotal, illustrative, descriptive, lacks rigour, is unsystematic, biased, impossible to replicate and not generalizable. This string of criticisms often emanates from a position where qualitative interviews and research and what they can accomplish are not well-understood. They are easily countered in the following ways.

A researcher might take material from qualitative interviews to illustrate a particular point, or describe some aspect of the behaviour discussed, but this is not the aim of the game. Examples and illustrations are not anecdotal, but systematically drawn from detailed analysis of the data, using the preferred analytic approach. It is the analysis and the cogency of the theoretical reasoning that underlies it that is the source of the generalizability of qualitative data. Findings from qualitative interviews are, then, not generalizeable in the way that quantitative research hopes to be, that is, drawing a sample on agreed criteria from a statistically defined population, and then generalizing from the findings from that sample to the broader population. A long debate has traced this meaning of generalization, immersed in the normative quantitative paradigm, with how qualitative findings can be generalized with different formulations, and there have been attempts to change the term to avoid this negative association (Gobo 2008). But it has been suggested that in general '. . . it is the quality of the theoretical inferences that are made out of qualitative data that is crucial to the assessment of generalisation' (Bryman 2001: 283).

Qualitative interviews are inherently impossible to replicate, since as we have seen in these chapters they are a social interaction with many elements coming into play. These include location and context, the physical and social space within which the interview takes place, power relations at the social and individual levels and a wide range of characteristics, predispositions, understandings and emotions of interviewer and interviewee – a complex social relationship with a long and evolving history (Crow and Pope 2008). The qualitative interviewer seeks to make the research process as transparent as possible, being both rigorous and systematic in this regard, and most importantly practises reflexivity in taking into account the potential and actual effects of all of the other factors that are involved (Bourdieu et al. 1999: 607, 608). This in fact is the major challenge for the individual qualitative researcher. A further criticism rooted in the paradigm wars of the 1980s suggests that qualitative interviewing is subjective, which is an irrelevant concern when subjectivity is often the focus and the vehicle for research using qualitative interviewing.

Andrea Doucet and Natasha Mauthner (2008) elaborate this latter point, and provide a fascinating history of feminist critiques of the qualitative interview, which includes critiques of claims for *feminist* interviews, and related to various feminist stances through time. The chapter demonstrates how the interview as undertaken by feminists has changed and adapted in response to some of the criticisms outlined here and to changing theoretical concerns and developments, highlighting the major contributions of feminist research to this process of development and change more generally.

Threats and challenges to qualitative interviewing can include methodological challenges. James Scheurich (1995, 1997), for example, offers a methodological challenge from a postmodern perspective, some elements of which have been superseded by their adaptation and incorporation into the development and evolution of qualitative interviewing suggested in these pages, and outlined in Doucet and Mauthner (2008) in the context of feminist research and theory. Two important related points made by Scheurich refer to language: first that language itself has inherent instability, with contested meanings, ambiguity and open-endedness, and is subject to endless reinterpretation so that second, what a question or answer means to the interviewer can easily mean something different to the interviewee. These points about language are used in a strong criticism of coding, thematic analysis and systemization of the data, which in his view leads to misrepresentation of the interview and interviewee in favour of the researcher's perspective derived from their (modernist) research training. But devastating as this critique seems to be, it does not mean abandoning interviews for Scheurich; rather he calls for a postmodern approach that re-visions the interview with these criticisms in mind, using reflexivity (researcher and researched), noting social positionality and recognizing the inherent indeterminacy as potential, offering 'new imaginaries of interviewing' (1997: 74–75).

Graham Crow (2012) outlines five further methodological challenges for social science research and so qualitative interviewing that can lead us into the next section, where we consider the future for qualitative interviewing. Crow first highlights the challenge of keeping up with and exploiting technological change, aspects of which were considered briefly in Chapter 4 (see too Hooley et al. 2012). The second challenge is enhancing research capacity in an integrated way, which refers to the way that mixed methods, methodological pluralism and collaboration in interdisciplinary teams are essential for moving such integration forward. The third refers to research ethics, which is a major ongoing issue, particularly important currently in relation to qualitative longitudinal and online methods; the fourth considers the democratization of social research, that is, expanding collaboration more widely to include participants who might be inclined to ask 'What's in it for us?' and feel over-researched (Clark 2008), as well as wider collaborations with partners beyond the academic field, including research centres and commercial organizations. Amid all this change and challenge Crow suggests a fifth challenge: that we need to keep a sense of purpose and of history, and not rush headlong into innovatory methods of research before assuring ourselves that it will result in answers for new research questions that are arising, and generate better quality data and analyses than our old methods. Reservations about the rush to innovation include questions about what innovation is and whether the rush is being fuelled by publishers and social media and by funders' requirements for social research to demonstrate impact, all influencing researchers to feel that they should be using new and exciting methods (Bengry-Howell et al. 2011).

One very general methodological challenge to social research was put forward by sociologists Mike Savage and Roger Burrows (2007). They suggested that the in-depth interview and the other basic method of sociological research, the survey, which had provided innovative and robust service in giving access to the 'social' for much of the twentieth century, are increasingly dated research methods that are unlikely to serve sociology well in the future. They point to the challenge to social researchers' expertise posed 'by the proliferation of 'social' transactional data which are now routinely collected, processed and analysed by a wide variety of private and public institutions' (885). In Savage and Burrows' responses to criticisms of that argument, they repeat and elaborate their message about 'knowing capitalism' by outlining some of its activities:

> Welcome to the world of 'knowing capitalism' (Thrift 2005): a world inundated with complex processes of social and cultural digitisation; a world in which commercial forces predominate; and a world in which we, as sociologists, are losing whatever jurisdiction we once had over the study of the 'social' as the generation, mobilization and analysis of social data become ubiquitous. (Savage and Burrows 2009: 763)

Their intention was not to generate despair but to urge sociologists and other social scientists to recognize the gravity of the challenge, to engage with and contribute to political debates over method and data and to get our hands dirty, to apply social theory to these steadily accumulating data acquired through surveillance and monitoring in pursuit of sociological knowledge, a position with which many contributors to the ensuing debate concurred (McKie and Ryan 2012; Murthy 2008; Webber 2009).

Future

An optimistic take on the future for qualitative interviewing picks up on elements in the 'strengths' and 'challenges' outlined here. Qualitative research is vibrant, alive and in demand in the interview and observation society (Atkinson and Silverman 1997; Gobo 2011; Mason 2002). It has survived massive cuts in public expenditure in the United Kingdom where research budgets have been reduced, or have disappeared entirely, without itself being disproportionately affected. This effect might have been expected if the normative quantitative paradigm had reasserted its power over the policy and public imaginary. Qualitative interviewing and research has a strong presence in research programmes, is seen as important in its own right, and is a key component of mixed method and evaluation studies. A stronger role is envisaged in the context of the current UK government localism agenda, where the emphasis is placed on communities generating resources and providing services (O'Connor 2011).

But all of this is not a cause for complacency, there have been dramatic changes in communication technology and qualitative interviewing must adapt if it is to survive. This does not mean pitting old methods against new, but it calls for constant renewal and making sure that we have the right tools for the job while also recognizing and supporting an enduring role for classic approaches, as argued by Crow quoted earlier in this chapter. A further issue in the rush to innovation is the claim by researchers that the method they use is democratic and new, when it in fact has a long history. One or two examples appear in Chapter 4, and a further example is the use of peer researchers, where an academic conducts research with people who live within, and are members of, a community. These peer/community researchers use their contacts and detailed knowledge of the community to help gather and understand information from and about their peers for the purposes of the research (see Chapter 2). But as one of us along with a colleague has pointed out (Edwards and Alexander 2011), working with peer and community researchers and regarding this as an alternative and empowering research paradigm is not new at all. It can be traced back to the influential thinker and town planner Patrick Geddes at the beginning of the twentieth century. His ideas for engaging local people in studying their own communities and the creation and ownership of data vested in local people inspired the community self-survey movement in the United Kingdom and United States during the interwar years (Bulmer 1984). The method also has potential for use in the changing research context of the future; we could think of the study of online communities in this respect.

There is a clear need to keep up with and exploit technological change which is currently being realized in a flourishing environment of innovation with a growing field of online research, including interviews, ethnography, focus groups and online analysis and reporting (Seale et al. 2010). Dhiraj Murthy (2008) builds on pioneering work in digital ethnography to critically examine the possibilities and problems of four technologies – online questionnaires, digital video (not new but being used in new ways, e.g. Senft 2008), social networking sites and blogs and their impacts on the research relationship. He concludes his analysis by arguing that new media and digital forms of 'old media' are additional, valuable methods in the social researcher's toolkit for qualitative interviewing.

Much of the debate about the perils and possibilities of the internet and the information revolution for social researchers centre around the future obsolescence of current offline methodological approaches such as the face-to-face qualitative interview (Savage and Burrows 2007, 2009), and the need to be aware of, familiar with and ready to exploit the possibilities that the internet offers in terms of potential for research and methodological development (Robinson and Schulz 2009).

Conclusion

Throughout this book we have provided information, suggestions and advice about qualitative interviews. Our basic approach can be summarized in a few points.

- The philosophical approach of a piece of research underpins understandings and leads to choices about:
  - what interviews are and how they can be used,
  - how the person being interviewed is positioned,
  - the types of interview to use,
  - the tools to use in the interview,
  - how many people to interview.
- Attention must be paid to the social context of the interview and concomitant:
  - meanings and social and power relations intersecting in socio-spatial and time/place dimensions of interviews,
  - power and emotional dynamics that shape interviews.

In the final chapter we hope to have brought encouragement to the aspiring qualitative interviewer that the method still has considerable mileage and much to offer social research, but that we must, as in our interviews, be flexible and responsive in order to meet the increasing challenges that confront us in the changing social and research environment.

Annotated bibliography

In this brief annotated bibliography we provide references to a range of books and edited collections that provide good discussions of qualitative interviewing, followed by methods-related journals that can be consulted for articles about interviewing.

Books and edited collections

Most general social research textbooks cover qualitative interview methods, but there are a number of introductory texts, books, handbooks and edited collections that focus specifically on qualitative interviews. The fact that several of these have been updated and republished in new editions attests to their popularity and enduring relevance.

Fielding, N. G. (ed.) (2009) *Interviewing II* (four volume set), Thousand Oaks, CA: London and New Delhi: Sage.
This is an authoritative reader that gathers together a comprehensive set of classic articles and chapters by key figures in the field of social research, with an emphasis on qualitative interviews. Volumes and sections range across epistemology, forms and designs, and practicalities and process.

Fontana, A. and Prokos, A. H. (2007) *The Interview: From Formal to Postmodern*, Walnut Creek, CA: Left Coast Press.
In this introductory text, Fontana and Prokos overview a range of approaches to interviewing from formal, through focused to unstructured, in the course of which they outline developments in perspectives over time towards an interview society. They conclude with a look at new trends and future developments.

Gubrium, J. F. and Holstein, J. A. (eds) (2002) *The SAGE Handbook of Interview Research: Context and Method*, Thousand Oaks, CA, London and New Delhi: Sage.

This handbook is a comprehensive collection with contributions from major figures in the field. It covers the standard forms of qualitative interviews, but is distinctive in having sections that focus on, respectively, particular social groups of interviewees (e.g. women, older people, elites) and settings or conditions for interviews (e.g. therapy, education, internet).

Gubrium, J. F. and Holstein, J. A. (eds) (2003) *Postmodern Interviewing*, Thousand Oaks, CA, London and New Delhi: Sage.

This is an influential collection of pieces concerned with postmodern interview practice. Contributions to the collection explore the way that the exchange between interviewer and interviewee/s – when, how and why questions are asked and stories constructed – is of significance. The collection as a whole conveys the variety of experimental possibilities of postmodern approaches for understanding and undertaking qualitative interviewing.

Hollway, W. and Jefferson, T. (2012) *Doing Qualitative Research Differently: Free Association Narrative and the Interview Method*, Thousand Oaks, CA, London and New Delhi: Sage, 2nd edn.

This book delineates a particular model of psychosocial interviewing developed by Hollway and Jefferson – the free association narrative interview, FANI, comprising two stages: (i) free association where the interviewee tells their own story in their own way, and (ii) structured narrative questions driven by the researcher.

King, N. and Horrocks, C. (2010) *Interviews in Qualitative Research*, Thousand Oaks, CA, London and New Delhi: Sage.

This introductory book discusses philosophies and explanation of concepts, alongside step-by-step practical advice about how to undertake various types of qualitative interviews in different settings and conditions. Phenomenological and narrative approaches receive particular attention.

Kvale, S. and Brinkmann, S. (2009) *InterViews: Learning the Craft of Qualitative Research Interviewing*, Thousand Oaks, CA, London and New Delhi: Sage, 2nd edn.

As part of a general introduction to interviewing, the second edition of this influential book identifies seven aspects of enabling knowing through the psychoanalytic research interview practice, including intensive individual case studies, open and non-directive modes of interviewing, interpretation of meaning to allow for ambiguity and contradiction, temporal intertwining of past, present and future, and emotional human interaction.

Merton, R. K., Fiske, M. and Kendall, P. L. (1990[1956]) *The Focused Interview: A Manual of Problems and Procedures*, New York: Free Press/ Macmillan.
Chapter 7 of this revised and updated version of Merton's classic 1956 text on qualitative interviewing guides the reader through the technique of group interviews specifically. In particular, Merton argues that a good focus group interview aims to cover range, specificity, depth and context for a topic through group interaction. The discussion of the advantages and disadvantages of the method remains telling.

Roulston, K. (2010) *Reflective Interviewing: A Guide to Theory and Practice*, London: Sage.
This introductory book has a strong emphasis on the connection between theory and interview methods. It also has a specific focus on reflexivity and subjectivity in the research process, with Roulston addressing various ways of practising reflexivity.

Rubin, H. J. and Rubin, I. S. (2011) *Qualitative Interviewing: The Art of Hearing Data*, Thousand Oaks, CA, London and New Delhi: Sage, 3rd edn.
An introductory text on interviewing stresses the importance of listening. Rubin and Rubin cover the stages prior to and following on the interview itself, using empirical examples to illustrate and demonstrate points.

Salmons, J. (ed.) (2011) *Cases in Online Interview Research*, Thousand Oaks, CA, London and New Delhi: Sage.
This book is a teaching resource that is useful to dip into for ideas about the gamut of computer-mediated means of conducting online interviews: how they can be mixed with other methods of research, how to use them and their strengths and limitations.

Seidman, I. (2006) *Interviewing as Qualitative Research: A Guide for Researchers in Education and the Social Sciences*, New York: Teachers College Press, 3rd edn.
This is a general text aimed largely at novice researchers that covers a range of interviewing approaches but with a particular focus on

phenomenology. Seidman gives attention to the obligations of researchers in their relationship with research participants, and stresses a collaborative partnership between researcher and research participant.

Spradley, J. P. (1979) *The Ethnographic Interview*, New York: Holt, Rinehart and Winston.

This is a classic methods text that stresses the search for meaning that people make of their lives through investigating tacit cultural knowledge and processes. Spradley presents a systematic, step-by-step, approach to ethnographic interviewing from locating an informant through to writing up. His categorization of types of questions and probes has been very influential.

Wengraf, T. (2001) *Qualitative Research Interviewing: Biographic Narratives and Semi-Structured Methods*, Thousand Oaks, CA, London and New Delhi: Sage.

This book puts forward a particular model of psychosocial interviewing with the aim of accessing participants' accounts of events and emotions – the biographical-narrative-interpretive methods: BNIM. Wengraf provides a practical guide for the interviewer in how to listen and facilitate through intra-narrative prompts, but not direct the interviewee's narrative.

Journals

There are several peer-refereed journals addressing various methodological approaches and techniques, including journals specializing in qualitative methods.

Forum: Qualitative Social Research / Forum Qualitative Sozialforschung

This open-access journal publishes a diverse mix of articles on aspects of qualitative methods, including many addressing aspects of interviewing, which is available at www.qualitative-research.net/index.php/fqs.

International Journal of Qualitative Methods

Assorted aspects of interviewing with a strong emphasis on reflexive subjectivity are a feature of this open-access journal, which is available at http://ejournals.library.ualberta.ca/index.php/IJQM/index.

Qualitative Inquiry

This subscription journal publishes articles concerned with emancipatory and experimental postmodern approach to qualitative research, including interviews. It is available at http://qix.sagepub.com/.

The International Journal of Social Research Methodology

Qualitative interviews in various forms are a recurrent topic of articles in standard issues of this subscription journal as well as special issues, which are available at www.tandf.co.uk/journals/tsrm.

Qualitative Research

This subscription journal often contains pieces on interviewing from an interpretive perspective in particular, and is available at http://qrj.sagepub.com/.

Online resources

www.ncrm.ac.uk

The National Centre for Research Methods is a hub and network of research groups conducting research and providing training in different areas of social science research. Their training programmes and sets of resources can prove useful in pursuing qualitative interviewing and other research methods.

www.socialsciences.manchester.ac.uk/morgancentre/realities/toolkits

A helpful series of practical guides on a range of research methods, including several different types of interviews. These were initially developed by researchers on the NCRM Realities node, but have now moved to the current site at the Morgan Centre for the Study of Relationships and Personal Life at Manchester University, where papers on new topics continue to be produced.

http://sru.soc.surrey.ac.uk

Social Research Update is an ongoing series of research guides published quarterly by the Department of Sociology, University of Surrey. The series includes reviews of many useful areas of social research methodology, including several types of interviews, and is provided free on application.

www.esds.ac.uk/qualidata/support/interviews

This is an ESDS Qualidata (now subsumed into the UK Data Service) teaching resource, *Exploring Diverse Interview Types*, using archive data sources to give examples of the interviews discussed. These include: qualitative structured, semi- and unstructured interviews; feminist, life history, oral history and psychosocial interviews.

www.wellesleyinstitute.com/publication/peer-research-in-action

A series of three working papers on peer research in action produced at the Wellesley Institute. A helpful brief pamphlet about the peer research method, giving advantages and disadvantages is at www.shu.ac.uk/_assets/pdf/hccj-ResearchMethodology.pdf.

www.timescapes.leeds.ac.uk

Timescapes was the first major qualitative longitudinal study funded in the United Kingdom and explored how personal and family relationships develop and change over time. Seven empirical projects covered the life course, and all used variants of qualitative interviews as well as other often innovatory methods. A Secondary Analysis project demonstrated the use of the *Timescapes* data and the project *Making the Long View* demonstrated the process of archiving data. The data generated in this study is archived in The Timescapes Archive making it available for use in teaching and research (www.timescapes.leeds.ac.uk/archive/). A list of publications emanating from this initiative is at www.timescapes.leeds.ac.uk/assets/files/Timescapes-publication-list.pdf.

Examples of studies using qualitative interviews cited in this book

Henderson, S., Holland, J., McGrellis, S., Sharpe, S. and Thomson, R. (2007) *Inventing Adulthoods: A Biographical Approach to Youth Transitions*, London: Sage.

A good example of a qualitative longitudinal study taking a biographical perspective and of mixing in-depth interviews with other methods (see Chapter 3 in this book). The study used in-depth interviews and other methods to follow young people's transitions into adulthood over the course of a decade. Henderson et al. spell out their biographical approach in chapter 2, and appendix 1 of their monograph details the study methods.

Jordan, B., Redley, M. and James, S. (1994) *Putting the Family First: Identities, Decisions, Citizenship*, London: UCL Press.

This study is based on individual and joint interviews with higher income couples with children, exploring how they make choices and decisions about employment. It provides a good example of an interpretive, interactionist perspective (see Chapters 2 and 3 in this book). In chapter 2, Jordan et al. show how the interaction between interviewee and interviewer during an interview generates data, and appendix A is a thoughtful description of the research process as a whole.

Ribbens McCarthy, J., Edwards, R. and Gillies, V. (2003) *Making Families: Moral Tales of Parenting and Step-Parenting*, Durham: sociologypress.

A study of resident, step and non-resident parents based on individual in-depth interviews, from an interpretive, constructionist perspective that focuses on meaning. Ribbens McCarthy et al. provide an extended discussion of the interview process in chapter 1 of the monograph, and the appendix discusses and reproduces the vignettes that formed part of the interview approach (see Chapter 5 in this book).

Walkerdine, V., Lucey, H. and Melody, J. (2001) *Growing Up Girl: Psychosocial Explorations of Gender and Class*, Basingstoke: Palgrave Macmillan.

This qualitative longitudinal study draws on in-depth interviews with middle-class and working-class girls over a 20 year period, and is a good example of research conducted from a psychosocial perspective. The methods used in the research are introduced in chapter 1, and in chapter 4 Walkerdine et al. discuss the extensive fieldnotes that they took describing their own thoughts and reactions to the interviews as part of their psychosocial approach (see Chapters 3 and 7 in this book).

References

Alastalo, M. (2008) 'The history of social research methods', in P. Alasuutari, L. Bickman and J. Brannen (eds) *The SAGE Handbook of Social Research Methods*, London: Sage.

Alderson, P. and Morrow, V. (2004) *Ethics, Social Research and Consulting with Children and Young People*, London: Barnardo's.

Anderson, J. (2004) 'Talking whilst walking: a geographical archaeology of knowledge', *Area*, 36(3): 254–261.

Ashford, S. and Timms, N. (1992) *What Europe Thinks: Study of Western European Values*, Dartmouth: Aldershot.

Ashmore, M. and Reed, D. (2000) 'Innocence and nostalgia in conversation analysis: the dynamic relations of tape and transcript', *Forum: Qualitative Social Research*, 1(3), Art. 3. Online publication accessed 7.4.12: www.qualitative-research.net/index.php/fqs/article/view/1020/2199.

Atkinson, P. (1997) 'Narrative turn or blind alley?', *Qualitative Health Research*, 7: 325–344.

Atkinson, P. and Hammersley, M. (1994) 'Ethnography and participant observation', in N. K. Denzin and Y. S. Lincoln (eds) *Handbook of Qualitative Research*, London: Sage.

Atkinson, P. and Silverman, D. (1997) 'Kundera's immortality: the interview society and the invention of self', *Qualitative Inquiry*, 3(3): 304–325.

Atkinson, P., Coffey, A., Delamont, S., Lofland, J. and Lofland, L. (2001) *Handbook of Ethnography*, London: Sage.

Back, L. (2010) *Broken Devices and New Opportunities: Re-Imagining the Tools of Qualitative Research*, National Centre for Research Methods Working Paper 08/10. Online publication accessed 6.4.12: http://eprints.ncrm.ac.uk/1579/1/0810_broken_devices_Back.pdf.

Backett, K. C. (1990) 'Studying health in families: a qualitative approach', in S. Cunningham-Burley and N. P. McKeganey (eds) *Readings in Medical Sociology*, London: Routledge.

Baker, S. E. and Edwards, R. (eds) (2012) *How Many Qualitative Interviews Is Enough? Expert Voices and Early Career Reflections on Sampling and Cases in Qualitative Research*, National Centre for Research Methods Review Paper. Online publication accessed 27.3.11: http://eprints.ncrm.ac.uk/2273/4/how_many_interviews.pdf.

Bampton, R. and Cowton, C. J. (2002) 'The e-interview', *Forum Qualitative Sozialforschung / Forum: Qualitative Social Research*, 3(2), Art. 9, http://nbn-resolving.de/urn:nbn:de:0114-fqs020295.

Bell, C. (1978) 'Studying the locally powerful: personal reflections on a research career', in C. Bell and S. Cencel (eds) *Inside the Whale*, Sydney: Pergamon.

Beneito-Montagut, R. (2011) 'Ethnography goes online: towards a user-centred methodology to research interpersonal communication on the internet', *Qualitative Research*, 11(6): 716–735.

Bengry-Howell, A., Wiles, R., Nind, M. and Crow, G. (2011) *A Review of the Academic Impact of Three Methodological Innovations: Netnography, Child-led Research and Creative Research Methods*, ESRC National Centre for Research Methods Working Paper, http://eprints.soton.ac.uk/194895/.

Bernard, H. R. (2000) *Social Research Methods: Qualitative and Quantitative Approaches*, Thousand Oaks, CA, London and New Delhi: Sage.

Bhaskar, R. A. (1989) *Reclaiming Reality: A Critical Introduction to Contemporary Philosophy*, London: Verso.

Bhavnani, K. K. (1993) 'Tracing the contours: feminist research and feminist objectivity', *Women's Studies International Forum*, 16(2): 85–104.

Bhopal, K. (1997) *Gender, 'Race' and Patriarchy*, Aldershot: Ashgate.

Biggs, C. L. (2003) 'Interviewing, power/knowledge, and social inequality', in J. F. Gubrium and J. A. Holstein (eds) *Postmodern Interviewing*, London: Sage.

Birch, M. and Miller, T. (2000) 'Inviting intimacy: the interview as therapeutic opportunity', *International Journal of Social Research Methodology*, 3(3): 189–202.

Bjornholt, M. and Farstad, G. R. (2012) '"Am I rambling?": on the advantages of interviewing couples together', *Qualitative Research*. Online publication accessed 3.11.12: http://qrj.sagepub.com/content/early/2012/10/05/1468794112459671.

Blackman, S. (1995) *Youth: Positions and Oppositions – Style, Sexuality and Schooling*, Aldershot: Avebury Press.

Bloor, M., Fincham, B. and Sampson, H. (2007) *Commissioned Inquiry into the Risk to Well-Being of Researchers in Qualitative Research*, Cardiff: QUALITI (NCRM). Accessed on 29.6.12: www.cardiff.ac.uk/socsi/qualiti/CIReport.pdf.

— (2010) 'Unprepared for the worst: risks of harm for qualitative researchers', *Methodological Innovations Online*, 5(1): 45–55.

Bornat, J. (2008) 'Biographical methods', in P. Alasuutari, L. Bickman and J. Brannen (eds) *The Sage Handbook of Social Research Methods*, London: Sage.

— *Oral History and Qualitative Research*, Timescapes Methods Guides Series No. 12, www.timescapes.leeds.ac.uk/assets/files/methods%20 guides/bornat_online.pdf.

Bourdieu, P., Accardo, A., Balzs, G., Beaud, S., Bonvin, F., Bourdieu, E., Bourgois, P., Broccolichi, S., Champagne, P., Christin, R., Faguer, J.-P., Garcia, S., Lenoir, R., Euvrard, F., Pialoux, M., Pinto, L., Podalydes, D., Sayad, A., Soulie, C. and Wacquant, L. J. D. (1999) *The Weight of the World: Social Suffering in Contemporary Society*, Cambridge: Polity.

Brannen, J. (1992) (ed.) *Mixing Methods: Qualitative and Quantitative Research*, Aldershot: Avebury.

— (2005) *Mixed Methods Research: A Discussion Paper*, ESRC NCRM Methods Review Papers NCRM/005: http://eprints.ncrm.ac.uk/89/1/MethodsReviewPaperNCRM-005.pdf.

Bryman, A. (1988) *Quantity and Quality in Social Research*, London: Routledge.

— (2001) *Social Research Methods*, Oxford: Oxford University Press.

Bulmer, M. (1984) *The Chicago School of Sociology: Institutionalisation, Diversity and the Rise of Sociological Research*, Chicago: University of Chicago Press.

Burgess, R. G. (1984) *In the Field: An Introduction to Field Research*, London: Allen & Unwin.

Chamberlayne, P., Bornat, J. and Wengraf, T. (2000) *The Turn to Biographical Methods in Social Science: Comparative Issues and Examples*, London: Routledge.

Chen, P. and Hinton, S. M. (1999) 'Realtime interviewing using the World Wide Web', *Sociological Research Online*, 4(3), www.socresonline.org.uk/4/3/chen.html.

Clark, A. and Emmel, N. (2010) 'Using walking interviews', NCRM Realities Toolkit 13. Available at http://eprints.ncrm.ac.uk/1323/1/13-toolkit-walking-interviews.pdf.

Clark, T. (2008) '"We're over-researched here!" Exploring accounts of research fatigue within qualitative research engagements', *Sociology* 42(5): 953–970.

Coffey, P. (1999) *The Ethnographic Self*, London: Sage.

Corbin, J. and Strauss, A. (2008) *Basics of Qualitative Research: Techniques and Procedures of Developing Grounded Theory*, Thousand Oaks: Sage, 3rd edn.

Cornwall, A. and Jewkes, R. (1995) 'What is participatory research?', *Social Science and Medicine*, 41(12): 1667–1676.

Cotterill, P. (1992) 'Interviewing women: issues of friendship, vulnerability and power', *Women's Studies International Forum*, 15: 593–606.

Cronin, A., Alexander, V. D., Fielding, J., Moran-Ellis, J. and Thomas, H. (2008) 'The analytic integration of qualitative data sources', in P. Alasuutari, L. Bickman and J. Brannen (eds) *The Sage Handbook of Social Research Methods*, London: Sage.

Crow, G. (2012) 'Methodological challenges for the 21st century', paper, www.sheffield.ac.uk/polopoly_fs/1.172803!/file/1120crow.pdf.

Crow, G. and Pope, C. (2008) 'The future of the research relationship', *Sociology* 42(5): 813–819.

Cussins, C. M. (1998) 'Ontological choreography: agency for women patients in an infertility clinic', in M. Berg and S. Mol (eds) *Differences in Medicine: Unraveling Practices, Techniques, and Bodies*, Durham NC: Duke University Press.

Davis, P. (2007) 'Storytelling as a democratic approach to data collection: interviewing children about reading', *Educational Research*, 49(2), 169–184.

Denzin, N. K. and Lincoln, Y. S. (2000) 'Introduction: the discipline and practice of qualitative research', in N. K. Denzin and Y. S. Lincoln (eds) *The SAGE Handbook of Qualitative Research*, London: Sage, 2nd edn.

— (2011) 'Introduction: the discipline and practice of qualitative research', in N. K. Denzin and Y. S. Lincoln (eds) *The SAGE Handbook of Qualitative Research*, London: Sage, 4th edn.

Dickson-Swift, V., James, E. L., Kippen, S. and Liamputtong, P. (2007) 'Doing sensitive research? What challenges do qualitative researchers face?', *Qualitative Research*, 7: 327–353.

Doucet, A. (1996) 'Encouraging voices: towards more creative methods for collecting data on gender and household labour', in L. Morris and E. S. Lyon (eds) *Gender Relations in Public and Private: New Research Perspectives*, Basingstoke: Macmillan Press.

— (2001) '"You see the need perhaps more clearly than I have": Exploring gendered processes of domestic responsibility', *Journal of Family Issues*, 22: 328–357.

Doucet, A. and Mauthner, N. (2008) 'Qualitative interviewing and feminist research', in P. Alasuutari, L. Bickman and J. Brannen (eds) *The SAGE Handbook of Social Research Methods*, London: Sage.

Duke, K. (2002) 'Getting beyond the "official line": reflections on dilemmas of access, knowledge and power in researching policy networks', *Journal of Social Policy*, 31(1): 39–60.

Duncan, S. and Edwards, R. (1999) *Lone Mothers, Paid Work and Gendered Moral Rationalities*, London: Macmillan.

Duncombe, J. and Jessop, J. (2007) '"Doing rapport" and the ethics of "faking friendship"', in M. Mauthner, M. Birch, J. Jessop and T. Miller (eds) *Ethics in Qualitative Research*, London: Sage.

Duncombe, J. and Marsden, D. (1993) 'Love and intimacy', *Sociology*, 27(2): 221–242.

Edwards, R. (1990) 'Connecting method and epistemology: a white woman interviewing black women', *Women's Studies International Forum*, 13(5): 477–490.

Edwards, R. and Alexander, C. (2011) 'Researching with peer/community researchers – ambivalences and tensions', in M. Williams and W. P. Vogt (eds) *The SAGE Handbook of Innovation in Social Research Methods*, London: Sage.

Edwards, R. and Mauthner, M. (2012) 'Ethics and feminist research: theory and practice', in T. Miller, M. Birch, M. Mauthner and J. Jessop (eds) *Ethics in Qualitative Research*, London: Sage, 2nd edn.

Edwards, R., Weller, S. and Baker, S. (2014) 'Generations and aspirations: young people's thinking about relationsips with siblings and hopes for their parents over time', in J. Holland and R. Edwards (eds) *Understanding Families over Time: Research and Policy*, Basingstoke: Palgrave.

Edwards, R., Hadfield, L., Lucey, H. and Mauthner, M. (2006) *Sibling Identity and Relationships: Sisters and Brothers*, Abingdon: Routledge.

Elliott, A. (2002) *Psychoanalytic Theory: An Introduction*, Durham, NC: Duke University Press.

Elwood, S. and Martin, D. (2000) 'Placing interviews: location and scales of power in qualitative research', *Professional Geographer*, 52: 649–657.

Ethnography and Education. (2013) 'Doing educational ethnography in an online world: methodological challenges, choices and innovations' 8(2): Special issue.

Ezzy, D. (2010) 'Qualitative interviewing as an embodied emotional performance', *Qualitative Inquiry*, 16(3): 163–170.

Ferrell, J. and Hamm, M. S. (1998) (eds) *Ethnography at the Edge: Crime, Deviance, and Field Research*, Boston: North Eastern University Press.

Finch, J. (1984) '"It's great to have someone to talk to": the ethics and politics of interviewing women', in C. Bell and H. Roberts (eds) *Social Researching*, London: Routledge & Kegan Paul.

— (1987) 'The vignette technique in survey research', *Sociology*, 21: 105–114.

Fitz, J. and Halpin, D. (1994) 'Ministers and mandarins: education research in elite settings', in G. Walford (ed.) *Researching the Powerful in Education*, London: UCL Press.

Freire, P. (2000[1970]) *Pedagogy of the Oppressed*, New York: Continuum.

Frith, H. (2000) 'Focusing on sex: using focus groups in sex research', *Sexualities* 3(3): 275–297.

Gabb, J. (2008) *Researching Intimacy in Families*, London: Palgrave Macmillan.

Game, A. (1997) 'Sociology's emotions', *Canadian Review of Sociology & Anthropology*, 34: 383–399.

Gauntlett, D. (2007) *Creative Explorations: New Approaches to Identities and Audiences*, London: Routledge.

Gibson, L. (2010) 'Using email interviews', NCRM Realities Toolkit 9. Available at http://eprints.ncrm.ac.uk/1303/1/09-toolkit-email-interviews.pdf.

Giddens, A. (1991) *Modernity and Self-identity: Self and Society in the Late Modern Age*, Cambridge: Polity Press.

— (2003) *Runaway World: How Globalisation Is Reshaping Our Lives*, Abingdon: Routledge.

Gill, S. and Goodson, I. (2011) 'Life history and narrative methods', in B. Somekh and C. Lewin (eds) *Theory and Methods in Social Research*, London: Sage, 2nd edn.

Gillies, V. (2004) 'Researching through working class personal networks: issues and dilemmas in bridging different worlds', in R. Edwards (ed.) *Social Capital in the Field: Researchers' Tales*, Families & Social Capital Research Group Working Paper No. 10, London: London South Bank University.

Gillies, V. and Edwards, R. (2012) 'Working with archived classic and community studies: illuminating past and present conventions around acceptable research practice', Special issue: 'Perspectives on working with archived textual and visual material in social research', G. Crow and R. Edwards (eds), *International Journal of Social Research Methodology*, 15(4): 321–330.

Glaser, B. G. and Strauss, A. (1967) *The Discovery of Grounded Theory: Strategies for Qualitative Research*, Chicago IL: Aldine.

Gobo, G. (2005) 'The renaissance of qualitative methods', *Forum: Qualitative Social Research*, 6(3), Art. 42, http://nbn-resolving.de/urn:nbn:de:0114-fqs0503420.

— (2007[2004]) 'Sampling, representativeness and generalizability', in C. Seale, G. Giampietro, J. F. Gubrium and D. Silverman (eds), *Qualitative Research Practice*, London: Sage.

— (2008) 'Re-conceptualizing generalization: old issues in a new frame', in P. Alasuutari, L. Bickman, and J. Brannen (eds) *The Sage Handbook of Social Research Methods*, London: Sage.

— (2011) 'Ethnography', in D. Silverman (ed.) *Qualitative Research*, London: Sage.

Greene, S. and Hogan, D. (eds) (2005) *Researching Children's Experience: Approaches and Methods*, London: Sage.

Gubrium, J. F. and Holstein, J. A. (2003a) 'From the individual interview to the interview society', in J. F. Gubrium and J. A. Holstein (eds) *Postmodern Interviewing*, London: Sage.

— (eds) (2003b) *Postmodern Interviewing*, London: Sage.

Guenette, F. L. and Marshall, E. A. (2009) 'Time line drawings: enhancing participant voice in narrative interviews on sensitive topics', *International Journal of Qualitative Methods*, 8(1). Online publication accessed 1.1.2012: http://ejournals.library.ualberta.ca/index.php/IJQM/article/view/3388/5200.

Guest, G., Bunch, A. and Johnson, L. (2006) 'How many interviews are enough? An experiment with data saturation and variability', *Field Methods*, 18(1): 59–82.

Hammersley, M. (2012) *What Is Qualitative Research?* London: Bloomsbury Academic.

Hanna, P. (2012) 'Using internet technologies (such as Skype) as a research medium: a research note', *Qualitative Research* 12(2): 239–242.

Harden, J., Backett-Milburn, K., Hill, M. and Maclean, A. (2010) 'Oh, what a tangled web we weave: Experiences of doing "multiple perspectives" research in families', *International Journal of Social Research Methodology*, 13(5), 441–452.

Harper, D. (2002) 'Talking about pictures: a case for photo elicitation', *Visual Studies*, 17(1): 13–26.

Heaphy, B. and Einarsdottir, A. (2012) 'Scripting civil partnerships: interviewing couples together and apart', *Qualitative Research*. Online publication accessed 4.11.12: www.esrc.ac.uk/my-esrc/grants/RES-062-23-1308/outputs/Read/49560ecf-ff42-4b88-aef9-e19c8061c93e.

Henderson, S., Holland, J., McGrellis, S., Sharpe, S. and Thomson, R. (2007) *Inventing Adulthoods: A Biographical Approach to Youth Transitions*, London: Sage.

Henwood, K., Shirani, F. and Finn, M. (2011) '"So you think we've moved, changed, the representation got more what?" Methodological and analytical reflections on visual (photo-elicitation) methods used in the Men as Fathers study', in P. Reavey (ed.) *Visual Methods in Psychology: Using and Interpreting Images in Qualitative Research*, London: Routledge.

Heyl, B. S. (2001) 'Ethnographic interviewing', in P. Atkinson, A. Coffey, S. Delamont, J. Lofland and L. Lofland (eds) *Handbook of Ethnography*, London: Sage.

Hine, C. (2001) *Virtual Ethnography*, London: Sage.

Hoffman, E. A. (2007) 'Open-ended interviews, power and emotional labour', *Journal of Contemporary Ethnography*, 36: 318–346.

Holland, J. (2007) 'Emotions and research', *International Journal of Social Research Methodology*, 10(3): 195–210.

— (2009) 'Emotions and research: some general and personal thoughts', in S. Weller and C. Caballero (eds) *Up Close and Personal: Relationships and Emotions 'Within' and 'Through' Research*, Families & Social Capital Research Group Working Paper No. 25, London South Bank University.

Holland, J. and Ramazanoglu, C. (1994) 'Coming to conclusions: power and interpretation in researching young women's sexuality', in M. Maynard and J. Purvis (eds) *Researching Women's Lives from a Feminist Perspective*, London: Taylor & Francis.

Holland, J., Thomson, R. and Henderson, S. (2006) *Qualitative Longitudinal Research: A Discussion Paper*, Families & Social Capital Working Paper Series No. 21, London South Bank University, www.lsbu.ac.uk/ahs/downloads/families/familieswp21.pdf.

Holland, J., Ramazanoglu, C., Sharpe, S. and Thomson, R. (2004) *The Male in the Head: Young People, Heterosexuality and Power*, London: the Tufnell Press.

Hollway, W. and Jefferson, T. (2012) *Doing Qualitative Research Differently: Free Association, Narrative and the Interview Method*, London: Sage, 2nd edn.

Holt, A. (2010) 'Using the telephone for narrative interviewing: a research note', *Qualitative Research* 10(1): 113–121.

Hooley, T., Wellens, J. and Marriott, J. (2012) *What Is Online Research?* London: Bloomsbury Academic.

Hubbard, G., Backett-Milburn, K. and Kemmer, D. (2001) 'Working with emotion: issues for the researcher in fieldwork and teamwork', *International Journal of Social Research Methodology*, 4: 119–137.

Ison, N. L. (2009) 'Having their say: email interviews for research data collection with people who have verbal communication impairment', *International Journal of Social Research Methodology*, 12(2): 161–172.

Jaggar, A. (1989) 'Love and knowledge: emotion in feminist epistemology', in S. Bordo and A. Jaggar (eds) *Gender/Body/Knowledge: Feminist Reconstructions of Being and Knowing*, New Brunswick: Rutgers University Press.

Jakobson, H. (2012) 'Focus groups and methodological rigour outside the minority world: making the method work to its strengths in Tanzania', *Qualitative Research* 12(2): 111–130.

James, N. and Busher, H. (2006) 'Credibility, authenticity and voice: dilemmas in online interviewing', *Qualitative Research* 6 (3): 403–420.

Johnson, R. B., Onwuegbuzie, A. J. and Turner, L. A. (2007) 'Towards a definition of mixed methods research', *Journal of Mixed Methods Research*, 1: 112–133.

Jones, S. H. (2005) 'Autoethnography: making the personal political', in N. Denzin and Y. Lincoln (eds) *Handbook of Qualitative Research*, Thousand Oaks, CA: Sage, 3rd edn.

Jordan, B., Redley, M. and James, S. (1994) *Putting the Family First: Identities, Decisions, Citizenship*, London: UCL Press.

Jorgenson, J. and Sullivan, S. (2010) 'Accessing children's perspectives through participatory photo interviews', *Forum: Qualitative Social Research*, 11(1), Art. 8, online publication accessed 4.4.12: www.qualitative-research.net/index.php/fqs/article/view/447/2890.

Kamberelis, G. and Dimitriadis, G. (2005) 'Focus groups: strategic articulations of pedagogy, politics, and inquiry', in N. Denzin and Y. Lincoln (eds) *Handbook of Qualitative Research*, Thousand Oaks, CA: Sage, 3rd edn.

Keightley, E., Pickering, M. and Allett, N. (2012) 'The self-interview: a new method in social science research', *International Journal of Social Research Methodology*, 15(6): 507–521.

Kenten, C. (2010) 'Narrating oneself: reflections on the use of solicited diaries with diary interviews', *Forum: Qualitative Social Research*, 11(2), Art. 16, online publication accessed 25.3.12: www.qualitative-research.net/index.php/fqs/article/view/13142989.

Kitzinger, J. (1994) 'The methodology of focus groups: the importance of interaction between research participants', *Sociology of Health and Illness*, 16(1): 103–121.

— (1995) 'Introducing focus groups', *British Medical Journal*, 311: 299–302.

Klatch, R. E. (1988) 'The methodological problems of studying a politically resistant community', *Community Studies in Qualitative Methodology*, 1: 73–88.

Kozinets, R. V. (2010) *Netnography: Doing Ethnographic Research Online*, London/Thousand Oaks, CA: Sage.

Kusenbach, M. (2003) 'Street phenomenology: the go-along as ethnographic research tool, *Ethnography* 4(3): 455–485.

Kvale, S. (1996) *Inter Views: An Introduction to Qualitative Research Interviewing*, London: Sage.

Lather, P. (1991) *Getting Smart: Feminist Research and Pedagogy with/in the Postmodern*, London: Routledge.

Lawler, S. (2002) 'Narrative in social research', in T. May (ed.) *Qualitative Research in Action*, London: Sage.

Lee, R. M. (2004) 'Recording technologies and the interview in sociology, 1920–2000', *Sociology*, 38(5): 800–889.

Letherby, G. (2003) *Feminist Research in Theory and Practice*, Buckingham: Open University Press.

Lewis, J. (2006) 'Making order out of a contested disorder: the utilisation of online support groups in social science research', *Qualitative Researcher* 3: 4–7.

Lucey, H., Melody, J. and Walkerdine, V. (2003) 'Project 4:21 Transitions to Womanhood: developing a psychosocial perspective in one longitudinal study', *International Journal of Social Research Methodology*, 6(3): 279–284.

Luker, K. (2008) *Salsa Dancing into the Social Sciences: Research in an Age of Info-Glut*, London: Harvard University Press.

MacNaughton, G., Rolfe, S. A. and Siraj-Blatchford, I. (2010) *Doing Early Childhood Research: International Perspectives on Theory and Practice*, London: Allen & Unwin.

Mahtani, M. (2012) 'Not the same difference: notes on mixed-race methodologies', in R. Edwards, S. Ali, C. Caballero and M. Song (eds) *International Perspectives on Racial and Ethnic Mixedness and Mixing*, Abingdon: Routledge.

Malinowski, B. (1922) *Argonauts of the Western Pacific: An Account of Native Enterprise and Adventure in the Archipelagoes of Melanesian New Guinea*, New York: Dutton.

Mann, C. and Stewart, F. (2000) *Internet Communication and Qualitative Research: A Handbook for Researching Online*, London: Sage.

Mason, J. (2002) *Qualitative Researching*, London: Sage, 2nd edn.

— (2006) *Six Strategies for Mixing Methods and Linking Data in Social Science Research*, Real Life Methods NCRM Node Working Paper. Online publication accessed 31.3.13: www.socialsciences.manchester.ac.uk/ morgancentre/realities/wps/4–2006–07-rlm-mason.pdf.

Mauthner, N. S. and Parry, O. (2009) 'Qualitative data preservation and sharing in the social sciences: on whose philosophical terms?', *Australian Journal of Social Issues*, 44(3): 289–305.

May, T. (1997) *Social Research: Issues, Methods and Process*, Buckingham: Open University Press, 2nd edn.

McGrellis, S., Henderson, S., Holland, J., Sharpe, S. and Thomson, R. (2000) *Through the Moral Maze: A Quantitative Study of Young People's Values*, London: the Tufnell Press.

McKie, L. and Ryan, L. (2012) 'Exploring trends and challenges in sociological research', *Sociology*, 46(6): 1–7, e-Special issue. doi:10.1177/0038038512452356.

Mead, G. H. (1935) *Mind, Self and Society*, Chicago: University of Chicago Press.

Medhurst, K. and Moyser, G. (1987) 'Studying a religious elite: the case of the Anglican Episcopate', in G. Moyser and M. Wagstaffe (eds) *Research Methods for Elite Studies*, London: Allen and Unwin.

Merton, R. K. (1987) 'The focused interview and focus groups: continuities and discontinuities', *Public Opinion Quarterly*, 51: 550–556.

Mickelson, R. A. (1994) 'A feminist approach to researching the powerful in education', in G. Walford (ed.) *Researching the Powerful in Education*, London: UCL Press.

Mikecz, R. (2012) 'Interviewing elites: addressing methodological issues', *Qualitative Inquiry*, 18: 482–493.

Miller, R. L. (2000) *Researching Life Stories and Family Histories*, London: Sage.

Miller, T. and Boulton, M. (2007) 'Changing constructions of informed consent: qualitative research and complex social worlds', *Social Science & Medicine*, 65: 2199–2211.

Mills, C. Wright (1959) *The Sociological Imagination*, New York: Oxford University Press.

Mishler, E. G. (1986) *Research Interviewing – Context and Narrative*, Cambridge MA: Harvard University Press.

Molloy, D. and Woodfield, K. with Bacon, J. (2002) *Longitudinal Qualitative Research Approaches in Evaluation Studies*, Working Paper No. 7, London: HMSO, http://research.dwp.gov.uk/asd/asd5/WP7.pdf.

Monrouxe, L. (2009) 'Solicited audio diaries in longitudinal narrative research: a view from inside', *Qualitative Research* 9(1): 81–103.

Moran-Ellis, J., Alexander, V. D., Cronin, A., Fielding, J. and Thomas, H. (2007) *Practice and Process in Integrating Methodologies (PPIMs)*, Methods Briefing 30. Online publication accessed 16.08.12: www.ccsr.ac.uk/methods/publications/#Briefings.

Moran-Ellis, J., Alexander, V. D., Cronin, A., Dickinson, M., Fielding, J., Sleney, J. and Thomas, H. (2006) 'Triangulation and integration: processes, claims and implications', *Qualitative Research* 6(1): 45–59.

Morgan, D. L. (1997) *Focus Groups and Qualitative Research*, *Sage Qualitative Research* Series 16, London: Sage, 2nd edn.

Morgan, D. L. and Spanish, M. T. (1984) 'Focus groups: a new tool for qualitative research', *Qualitative Sociology*, 7(3): 253–270.

Morse, J. (1994) 'Designing funded qualitative research', in N. K. Denzin and Y. S. Lincoln (eds) *Handbook of Qualitative Research*, London: Sage.

Murthy, D. (2008) 'Digital ethnography: an examination of the use of new technologies for social research', *Sociology* 42(5): 837–855.

Neale, B., Henwood, K. and Holland, J. (2012) 'Researching lives through time: an introduction to the Timescapes approach', *Qualitative Research* 12(1): 4–15.

Nind, M. (2008) *Conducting Qualitative Research with People with Learning, Communication and Other Disabilities: Methodological Challenges*, ESRC National Centre for Research Methods Review Paper. Online publication accessed 29.3.13: http://eprints.ncrm.ac.uk/491/1/MethodsReviewPaperNCRM-012.pdf.

Oakley, A. (1981) 'Interviewing women: a contradiction in terms', in H. Roberts (ed.) *Doing Feminist Research*, London: Routledge.

O'Connor, W. (2011) 'What's new? Reflections on current developments in qualitative social research', presentation at Social Research Association Annual Conference, www.thesra.org.uk/documents/pdfs/sra_annual_conference_2011_presentations/o%27connor.pdf.

O'Donnell, K. (2003) *Postmodernism*, Oxford: Lion Publishing.

Opdenakker, R. (2006) 'Advantages and disadvantages of four interview techniques in qualitative research', *Forum Qualitative Sozialforschung/Forum: Qualitative Social Research*, 7(4), Art. 11, online publication accessed 3.11.12: www.qualitative-research.net/index.php/fqs/article/view/175/391.

Overlien, C., Aronsson, K. and Hyden M. (2005) 'The focus group interview as an in-depth method? Young women talking about sexuality', *International Journal of Social Research Methodology*, 8(4): 331–344.

Park, R. and Burgess, E. (1925) *The City*, Chicago: University of Chicago Press.

Payne, G. (2006) *Social Divisions*, Basingstoke: Palgrave Macmillan, 2nd edn.

Peek, L. and Fothergill, A. (2009) 'Using focus groups: lessons from studying daycare centers, 9/11 and Hurricane Katrina', *Qualitative Research*, 9(1): 31–59.

Phillips, R. (1998) 'The politics of history: some methodological and ethical dilemmas in elite-based research', *British Educational Research Journal*, 24(1): 5–19.

Phoenix, A. (1994) 'Practising feminist research: the intersection of gender and "race" in the research process', in M. Maynard, and J. Purvis (eds) *Researching Women's Lives from a Feminist Perspective*, London: Taylor & Francis.

Porter, S. (2002) 'Critical realist ethnography', in T. May (ed.) *Qualitative Research in Action*, London: Sage.

Ramazanoglu, C. with Holland, J. (2002) *Feminist Methodology: Challenges and Choices*, London: Sage.

Reay, D. and Lucey, H. (2002) '"I don't really like it here but I don't want to be anywhere else": children and inner city council estates', *Antipode*, 32(4): 410–428.

Reynolds, T. (2004) '"Insider/outsider" Caribbean researcher: exploring social capital and access in the field', in R. Edwards (ed.) *Social Capital in the Field: Researchers' Tales*, Families & Social Capital Research Group Working Paper No. 10, London: London South Bank University.

Ribbens McCarthy, J., Edwards, R. and Gillies, V. (2003) *Making Families: Moral Tales of Parenting and Step-Parenting*, Durham: Sociologypress.

Riessman, C. K. (1993) *Narrative Analysis*, Qualitative Research Methods Volume 30, London/New Delhi: Sage.

— (2001) 'Analysis of personal narratives', in J. F. Gubrium and J. A. Holstein (eds) *Handbook of Interview Research*, Thousands Oaks, CA: Sage.

Robinson, L. and Schulz, J. (2009) 'New avenues for sociological inquiry: evolving forms of ethnographic practice', *Sociology*, 43(4): 685–698.

Rosenthal, G. (2004) 'Biographical research', in C. Seale, G. Gobo, J. F. Gubrium and D. Silverman (eds) *Qualitative Research Practice*, London: Sage.

Ross, K. (2001) 'Political elites and the pragmatic paradigm: notes from a feminist researcher – in the field and out to lunch', *International Journal of Social Research Methodology*, 4(2): 155–166.

Ross, N. J., Renold, E., Holland, S. and Hillman, A. (2009) 'Moving stories: using mobile methods to explore the everyday lives of young people in public care', *Qualitative Research*, 9(5): 605–623.

Sampson, H., Bloor, M. and Fincham, B. (2008) 'A price worth paying? Considering the "cost" of reflexive research methods and the influence of feminist ways of doing', *Sociology*, 42(5): 919–933.

Savage, M. (2010) *Identities and Social Change in Britain since 1940: The Politics of Method*, Oxford: Oxford University Press.

Savage, M. and Burrows, R. (2007) 'The coming crisis of empirical sociology', *Sociology* 41(5): 885–899.

— (2009) 'Some further reflections on the coming crisis of empirical sociology', *Sociology* 43(4): 762–772.

Scheurich, J. J. (1995) 'A postmodernist critique of research interviewing', *Qualitative Studies in Education*, 8(3): 239–252.

— (1997) *Research Method in the Postmodern*, London: Falmer Press.

Seale, C., Charteris-Black, J., MacFarlane, A. and McPherson, A. (2010) 'Interviews and internet forums: a comparison of two sources of qualitative data', *Qualitative Health Research*, 20(5): 595–606.

Senft, T. M. (2008) *Camgirls: Celebrity and Community in the Age of Social Networks*, New York: Peter Lang Publishing.

Séror, J. (2005) 'Computers and qualitative data analysis: papers, pens and highlighters vs. screen, mouse and keyboard', *TESOL Quarterly*, 29(2): 321–328.

Sheller, M. and Urry, J. (2006) 'The new mobilities paradigm', *Environment and Planning A* 38: 207–226.

Shepherd, N. (2003) 'Interviewing online: qualitative research in the network(ed) society', paper presented at the AQR Qualitative Research Conference, 16–19 July, Sydney, Australia. http://espace.library.uq.edu.au/eserv/UQ:10232/ns_qrc_03.pdf.

Skeggs, B. (1997) *Formations of Class and Gender: Becoming Respectable*, London: Sage.

Smithson, J. (2000) 'Using and analysing focus groups: limitations and possibilities', *International Journal of Social Research Methodology*, 3(2): 103–119.

Snee, H. (2008) Web 2.0 as a social science research tool, ESRC Government Placement Scheme, The British Library, www.restore.ac.uk/orm/futures/Web_2.0_final__v3.pdf.

Sparkes, A. C. (2000) 'Autoethnography and narratives of self: reflections on criteria in action', *Sociology of Sport Journal*, 17: 21–43.

Spradley, J. P. (1979) *The Ethnographic Interview*, Fort Worth, TX: Harcourt Brace.

Stacey, K. and Vincent, J. (2011) 'Evaluation of an electronic interview with multimedia stimulus materials for gaining in-depth responses from professionals', *Qualitative Research* 11(5): 605–624.

Stephens, N. (2007) 'Collecting data from elites and ultra elites: telephone and face-to-face', *Qualitative Research* 7(2): 203–216.

Stewart, K. and Williams, M. (2005) 'Researching online populations: the use of online focus groups for social research', *Qualitative Research* 5(4): 395–416.

Stockdale, A. (2002) 'Tools for digital audio recording in qualitative research', *Social Research Update*, 38 (Autumn). Online publication accessed 6.4.12: http://sru.soc.surrey.ac.uk/SRU38.html.

Sturges, J. E. and Hanrahan, K. J. (2004) 'Comparing telephone and face-to-face qualitative interviewing: a research note', *Qualitative Research* 4(1): 107–118.

Takhar, J. (2009) 'Covering up and revealing: reflecting on emotions in research with South Asian women', in S. Weller and C. Caballero (eds) *Up Close and Personal: Relationships and Emotions 'Within' and 'Through' Research*, Families & Social Capital Research Group Working Paper No. 25, London South Bank University.

Teddlie, C. and Tashakkori, A. (2010) 'Overview of contemporary issues in mixed methods research', in A. Tashakkori and C. Teddlie (eds) *Sage Handbook of Mixed Methods in Social and Behavioural Research*, Thousand Oaks, CA: Sage, 2nd edn.

Thomas, W. I. and Znaniecki, F. (1958[1918–20]) *The Polish Peasant in Europe and America*, New York: Dover Publications.

Thompson, P. (2008) 'Life stories, history and social change', in R. Edwards (ed.) *Researching Lives Through Time: Time, Generation and Life Stories*, Timescapes Working Paper No. 1 www.timescapes.leeds.ac.uk/assets/files/timescapes/WP1-Researching-Lives-Through-Time-June-2008.pdf.

Thompson, P. (with T. Lummis and T. Wailey) (1983) *Living the Fishing*, London: Routledge and Kegan Paul.

Thomson, R. and Holland, J. (2005) '"Thanks for the memory": memory books as a methodological resource in biographical research', *Qualitative Research*, 5(2): 201–219.

Thomson, R., Hadfield, L., Kehily M. J. and Sharpe, S. (2012) 'Acting up and acting out: encountering children in a longitudinal study of mothering', *Qualitative Research*, 12(2): 186–201.

Thrift, N. (2005) *Knowing Capitalism*, London: Sage.

Tong, R. (2009 3rd edn) *Feminist Thought: A More Comprehensive Introduction*, Boulder, CO: Westview Press.

Valentine, G. (1999) 'Corporeal geographies of consumption', *Environment and Planning D: Society and Space*, 17(3): 329–351.

Walkerdine, V., Lucey, H. and Melody, J. (2002) 'Subjectivity and qualitative method', in T. May (ed.) *Qualitative Research in Action*, London: Sage.

Wall, S. (2006) 'An autoethnography on learning about autoethnography', *International Journal of Qualitative Methods*, 5(2), Art. 9. Retrieved 16.08.12: www.ualberta.ca/~iiqm/backissues/5_2/PDF/wall.pdf.

Wallman, S. (1984) *Eight London Households*, London and New York: Tavistock Publications.

Watts, J. H. (2008) 'Emotions, empathy and exit: reflections on doing ethnographic qualitative research on sensitive topics', *Medical Sociology Online*, 3(3): 3–14.

Webber, R. (2009) 'Response to "The coming crisis of empirical sociology": an outline of the research potential of administrative and transactional data', *Sociology* 43(1): 169–178.

Weeks, J., Heaphy, B. and Donovan, C. (2001) *Same Sex Intimacies: Families of Choice and Other Life Experiments*, London and New York: Routledge.

Wengraf, T. (2001) *Qualitative Research Interviewing: Biographic Narrative and Semi-Structured Methods*, Thousand Oaks, CA, London and New Delhi: Sage.

Wengraf, T. with Chamberlayne P. (2006) *Interviewing for Life Histories, Lived Situations and Personal Experience: The Biographic-Narrative-Interpretive Method (BNIM). Short Guide to BNIM Interviewing and Interpretation*. Available from tom@wengraf.com.

Whyte, W. F. (1993[1943]) *Street Corner Society: The Social Structure of an Italian Slum*, Chicago: University of Chicago Press, 4th edn.

— (1996a) 'Qualitative sociology and deconstructionism', *Qualitative Inquiry*, 2(2): 220–226.

— (1996b) 'Facts, interpretations, and ethics in qualitative inquiry', *Qualitative Inquiry*, 2(2): 242–244.

Wiles, R. (2012) *What Are Qualitative Research Ethics?* London: Bloomsbury.

Wiles, R., Heath, S., Crow, G. and Charles, V. (2005) *Informed Consent in Social Research: A Literature Review*, National Centre for Research Methods Review Paper. Online publication accessed 8.4.12: http://eprints.ncrm.ac.uk/85/1/MethodsReviewPaperNCRM-001.pdf.

Williams, M. (2000) *Sciences and Social Sciences*, London: Sage.

Williams, M. and Vogt W. P. (eds) (2011) *The Sage Handbook of Innovation in Social Research Methods*, London: Sage.

Winter, K. (2012) 'Ascertaining the perspectives of young children in care: case studies in the use of reality boxes', *Children & Society* 26: 368–380.

Yanow, D. and Schwartz-Shea, P. (2006) *Interpretation and Method: Empirical Research Methods and the Interpretive Turn*, New York: M.E. Sharp.

Index